DATE DUE			
OCT 16 1980			
DEC 4 1980			
FEB 26 1981			
APR - 1 1981			
SEP 10 1981			
AUG 4 1982			
SEP 28 1982			
DEC 30 1983			
SEP 18 1984			

WILLIAMSTOWN PUBLIC LIBRARY

Hunting
Whitetail
Deer

Hunting Whitetail Deer

Robert E. Donovan

Winchester Press

Copyright © 1978 by Robert E. Donovan

All rights reserved

Library of Congress Cataloging in Publication Data

Donovan, Robert E.
    Hunting whitetail deer.

    Includes index.
    1. White-tailed deer hunting.   I. Title.
SK301.D62   799.2'77'357   77-26890
ISBN 0-87691-257-9
9 8 7 6 5 4 3 2 1

Published by Winchester Press
205 East 42nd Street
New York, N.Y. 10017

WINCHESTER is a Trademark of Olin Corporation used
by Winchester Press, Inc. under authority and control
of the Trademark Proprietor

Printed in the United States of America

DEDICATION

To Kevin, Kara, and Peg:

The former are my prospective hunting and
fishing partners and the latter puts up with the
muddy boots, smelly fish, and grouse feathers.

Foreword

I spent many autumns in the woods before I got my first deer. So many, in fact, that I'm too embarrassed to admit the exact number. That was many years ago, and I did not have the advantage of a teacher to speed my learning process. I had to learn the slow way — by trial and error. I eventually learned to pick two stands in each area that I planned to hunt so that I'd be ready if the wind was blowing from an unexpected direction. I eventually learned to make sure that I was plenty comfortable before settling down in my stand so that I wouldn't fidget from discomfort and scare the deer. I eventually learned what kind of sights I needed on my rifle so that I would have the right sights for any hunting condition.

But learning that way was a slow process. I sincerely hope that this book will shorten that learning process for anyone else taking up the sport. I personally enjoy the time that I spend afield whether my hunt is successful or not. But too long a dry spell can sure make a fellow think that he should have taken up tennis. This book is intended to prevent any such long dry spells.

In addition to aiding the beginner, I think that this volume will also prove interesting and useful to the advanced hunter. Maybe it will encourage him to try a technique that he hasn't tried before, such as cresting. Maybe it will encourage him to try a weapon that he hasn't tried before, such as a muzzle-loading rifle. For both the beginner and the advanced hunter, this book is intended to be a handy one-stop reference on whitetail deer hunting containing virtually all the information on ballistics, butchering, and other subjects that the hunter is likely to need. In the few cases where the needed information would be too voluminous to include here, the reader is given a specific reference to another book.

There is also information included in this volume on the natural history of the deer and on his biology and physical characteristics. I suppose that some of this information isn't needed from a purely utilitarian deer-hunting point of view. But I think that most hunters are interested in their quarry not simply as quarry and table fare. They are also interested in game animals as creatures with which we share this limited planet and as creatures without whom this world would be a much poorer place to live.

So much for what I think this book is and what I intended it to be. Maybe I was successful in my effort; maybe I wasn't. You, the reader, must be the judge of that. Besides, I really do have to stop writing now. My dog just came over and laid her chin in my lap and that reminds me that today is the last day of quail season. I know about a little creek that runs through a grown-over field not too far from here, and I expect that I should walk the banks of that creek with my 20-gauge side-by-side one last time before the season closes. So I better be going. Good luck with your deer hunting — see you afield.

Robert E. Donovan
Lynchburg, Virginia
February, 1978

Contents

Part One

The Animal

1

A Brief History

"This Island had many goodly woods full of
Deere, Conies, Hares and Fowle, even in the
midst of summer in incredible abundance."
Capt. Arthur Barlowe describing Roanoke Island July 2, 1584

The ancestry of the North American whitetail deer is
lost in the murky depths of prerecorded history. Unlike
the elk, moose, and caribou which closely resemble certain European members of the deer family (Cervidae),
the whitetail deer has no close European relatives. This
fact leads scientists to believe that the ancestors of our
whitetail deer made the transition to this continent between 15 and 20 million years ago during the Miocene
epoch. In the ensuing millions of years, these deer have

evolved into a unique species, one unlike the elk, moose, and caribou, who made the transition comparatively recently and have had little time for significant evolutionary changes.

The exact form of the early deer is unknown. But whatever else these early deer may have been, they must have been tough and adaptable to withstand the climatic upheavals and predatory onslaughts to which they were subjected. The deer in North America have survived several ice ages and predation by saber-toothed tigers, pumas, wolves, and man.

The Mound Builders of the Mississippi Valley were among the first known human inhabitants of North America. Excavations of the ruins of their civilization indicate that the whitetail deer played a central role in their lives. At site after site, the most common bones found in the excavations are those of the whitetail deer. The deers' bones were fashioned into various kitchen and garden utensils, and deer hides were used for clothing and moccasins. Even in Southwest and Central America, the whitetail deer played a vital role in Indian life, and most of the few remaining Aztec manuscripts are written on buckskin.

When the white man first came to the New World, one of the things that most impressed him was the prevalence of game animals, especially deer. The deer are mentioned in the journal of Henry Hudson's *Half Moon* (1609), in George Percy's *Observations* of the Jamestown settlement, and in many other journals and diaries of English, Spanish, and Dutch settlers of the New World. Samuel Champlain, describing the lake that later came to bear his name, wrote on July 3, 1609, "There are many pretty islands here, low, and with very fine woods and meadows, with abundance of fowl and such animals of the chase as stags, fallow-deer, fawns, roe-bucks, bears and others which swim from the mainland to these islands."

Early records concerning the number of deer taken and the relative importance of venison in the colonial diet and economy are sketchy. It is certain, however, that venison was more important than beef in the colonial diet in the sixteenth, seventeenth, and much of the eighteenth century. In certain parts of the country, venison constituted the primary source of meat even 'through the nineteenth century. Colonial records indicate that in Florida during the 1750s whitetail deer hides traded for use as leather exceeded the monetary value of all other traded commodities combined. The annual export of hides from Charles Town during the period 1739 to 1762 fluctuated between 131,000 and 355,000 pounds depending on hunter luck and the state of local warfare. These figures indicate a rather sizable deer harvest when one considers that a typical hide weighs about one-and-a-half pounds. In 1786, Quebec exported 132,271 deerskins valued at £25,905. Deerskins were so widely accepted during the 1760s that they were taken in payment at a standard rate of about eighteen pence per pound "in the hair."

An interesting illustration of the negotiability of deer hides is provided by the attempt in 1784 to establish a sovereign State of Franklin in a goodly chunk of what is now western Tennessee. The salaries of the civil officers were established as 1,000 deerskins per year for the governor, 500 deerskins per year for the chief justice, and specified numbers of smaller pelts for lesser officials. This same act pegged the rate of exchange at six shillings per deer hide, which was up considerably from the eighteen-pence-per-hide rate of the 1760s, and leads one to conclude that the early settlers of this continent were no more adept at dealing with inflation than we are today.

As the human population of the country grew and the frontier expanded, the strain on the deer population grew greater. Many a logging camp and railroad crew derived its meat subsistence from venison. Market hunting grew in importance and wild-game markets sprang up in major cities. States with large deer herds became venison exporters. It is reported that in December, 1872, a single freight car left Litchfield, Minnesota, with 12,000 pounds of venison headed for Boston. Improved firearms and the ready market for venison made market hunting so lucrative that many hunters got into the act on a large scale. In 1860, a father-son team in Sherburne County, Minnesota, reportedly killed a whopping 6,000 deer for the market.

It was becoming increasingly obvious that something had to be done to protect the whitetail deer from extermination. As early as the middle 1600s, the deer populations around Plymouth and Rhode Island Colonies was declining, and by the late 1800s the whitetail had been driven from much of his former range.

Early efforts to regulate hunting met with considerable resistance. This was in part a reflection of the independent and self-reliant attitude of the colonists and pioneers. It was also a reflection of the pioneers' attitude that the game on the land was there for the taking and the state had no business interfering. Landowners, in particular, resented being told that they could not shoot "their own" deer on their own land. Historically, of course, wild game was not considered the property of the landowner. In England, the deer belonged to the Crown, and woe to the individual who was caught poaching.

Up until the time of the *Charter of the Forest,* an amendment

6

to the *Magna Carta* enacted during the reign of Henry III in 1217, the penalty for killing the "King's Royal Deer" was death. The *Charter of the Forest* banned the death penalty for poaching and contained this relatively mild and enlightened provision for poachers:

> Henceforth no one shall lose life or limbs on account of our hunting rights; but if anyone is arrested taking our venison, let him redeem himself by a heavy payment if he has anything with which to redeem himself. And if he has nothing with which to redeem himself, let him lie in our prison for a year and a day. And if, after the year and a day, he can find sureties, let him be freed from prison; but if he cannot, let him abjure the realm of England.

Pretty stiff penalties by today's standards!

The first colony to establish a closed season on deer was Rhode Island in 1646. This was followed by similar enactments in Massachusetts (1694), Connecticut (1698), and New York (1705). These laws were enforced in a hit-or-miss manner and achieved only marginal success. By and large, the laws were considered a minor nuisance at most and were commonly ignored by the colonists and frontiersmen. As a result, deer populations continued to decline. Finally, in the late 1800s, it became clear that the laws had to be enforced if the whitetail deer were to survive. The last territory to pass a closed-season law was Oklahoma in 1890, and the period 1890–1910 saw a general improvement in conservation-law enforcement. The public was made aware of the importance of conservation through the efforts of such men as Teddy Roosevelt, and by 1920 it was apparent that the whitetail deer was making a comeback. The national herd size has increased fairly steadily from a low of about half a million in 1900 to more than 15 million deer

Opposite:
1–1   Early conservation laws were either not strict enough, not enforced, or both. The whitetail deer population in the United States declined steadily into the early 1900s. The upper photograph shows a Wisconsin hunting scene circa 1880. Thirty-five years later, the situation had not changed much as indicated by the lower photograph which depicts a 1915 scene in Minnesota. Note the lack of discrimination in both pictures with respect to the age and sex of the deer killed. (Courtesy Minnesota Historical Society)

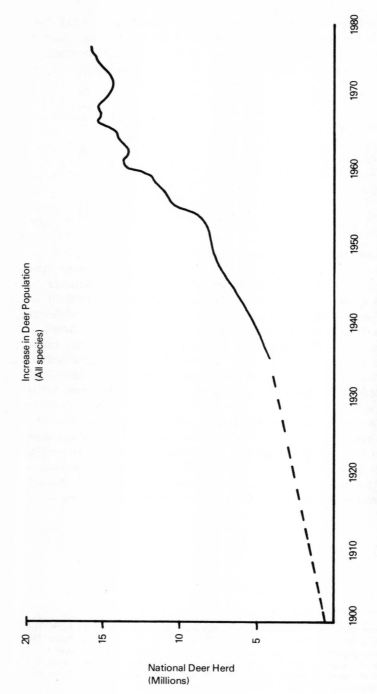

1-2   The national deer herd hit an all time population low sometime around the turn of the century. It has been estimated that there were only approximately 500,000 deer of all species in the United States in 1900. Better conservation laws, stricter enforcement, and increased public concern have combined to reverse the declining population trend and today there are over 15 million deer of all species (mule deer, whitetails, blacktails, and Sitka) in the United States. In recent years, whitetails have accounted for about 76% of the total.

of all species today. In recent years, some 76 percent of all deer in the United States have been whitetails, the remainder being mule deer and its blacktail and Sitka subspecies. Though some people say there are more whitetail deer in North America now than there were when the first European settlers arrived, we would find it hard to prove or disprove the theory since the herd size in precolonial times is quite difficult to estimate accurately. The estimate must be made based on present-day deer densities in fairly virgin or untouched areas and by estimating the conditions of vegetation that existed before the colonists arrived. In addition, the differences in predation between present and precolonial times must be considered. Some experts have placed the figure of the precolonial herd size as high as 40 million. Whatever the original national herd size was, it has increased dramatically in the last eighty years.

The previously discussed conservation laws are partly responsible for the increased number of deer. But in addition, some of the ways in which man has upset the balance of nature have worked to the deer's advantage. The puma, which used to range as far east as New York and was the deer's worst enemy, has been pushed back into a small fraction of its former range. The wolf, a fierce predator capable of decimating entire deer herds during periods of heavy snow, is now seen only occasionally in the northeastern United States even though it once ranged widely over this entire area. Man's logging and farming, and even his forest fires, have often worked to the long-term advantage of the whitetail deer. In virgin timber stands with thick foliage canopies and no low-lying brush or grass, deer have difficulty finding enough food. Areas that are cleared by logging or fires are recovered initially with young trees and brush which provide deer with the necessary browse. Some experts believe that the decline of the deer population in the Adirondacks is attributable to the "forever wild" clause of the New York State Constitution, which prohibits logging operations in the Adirondack Forest Preserve. As the trees mature, low-lying plants and branches disappear, and the carrying capacity of the range markedly decreases.

In spite of occasional conflicts such as this between the desire to maintain wild forest lands and the desire to improve deer habitat, it does appear that modern conservation programs have been effective in preserving or rebuilding the whitetail deer herds. With continued wise herd management and with continued attention to the needs of the animal, the whitetail deer herd in this country should continue to increase and to be a national asset for years to come.

2

Distribution
and Physical
Characteristics

It is a warm spring day toward the end of May. The
ground is damp, and raindrops bead the fresh and
brilliant leaves of another Adirondack spring. Black bil-
lowy rain clouds slip silently off toward Vermont, and
sunlight reflects from the recently showered mountains.
In a clearing high on a mountainside, a whitetail doe is
grazing on some freshly sprouted leaves. Now her head
jerks up, and she stares intently down the hill. She
stares for a moment, and then goes back to her eating.
Suddenly she feels a spasm in her abdomen, and a com-
pelling sense of urgency overtakes her. Nervously, she
walks over to a nearby clump of bushes, circles it once,
tests the air, again stares down the hill, and finally lies
down in a spot of shade. Her time to fawn has come.
She lies still for fifteen or twenty minutes. Then her abdomen begins to heave in convulsions that seem violent
for so frail an animal. But the convulsions soon stop
and she lies more relaxed now. She raises her head and
turns as if to lick herself. But it is not herself that she is
so intent on licking. Immediately behind her hindquar-

ters lies a wet and trembling newborn fawn. In these brief moments of birth, one more fawn has made the rude and traumatic transition from warm, dark, quiet, and soft to cold, bright, noisy, and hard. Far below, an occasional car zips by on Highway 10, and its occupants are completely unaware of the dramatic and reassuring event that has just occurred high on the mountain above them. It is an event that is repeated thousands of times over within a period of weeks in the surrounding mountains as the Adirondack whitetail deer herd witnesses the birth of the new fawns that will help insure the herd's survival in the years to come.

Distribution

A game biologist could tell you without even examining this newborn fawn that its biological designation is *Odocoileus virginianus*. If your biologist is really sharp, he can also tell you that there are approximately thirty subspecies of whitetail deer in North America, and that based on the place of birth of the just-described fawn, in New York, it is probably of the subspecies *Borealis*. A more complete designation for this deer would be *Odocoileus virginianus borealis*, or *O.V. borealis* for short.

Biologists have isolated thirty subspecies of whitetail deer, and one subspecies or another is found in nearly every part of North America. Whitetail deer range from the Atlantic to Pacific coasts and from the Isthmus of Panama in the south to approximately 55 degrees north latitude in parts of Canada. In some cases, where the boundary between subspecies is a major geographic barrier, such as a river or a mountain range, the line of demarcation is distinct and the subspecies are easily distinguished. In other cases, the boundaries are more difficult to define, the subspecies overlap, and interbreeding takes place. The situation is further complicated by the extensive transplanting that has been undertaken in some areas by state conservation agencies. For example, deer have been transplanted into northern Georgia from Michigan, Montana, Mississippi, Texas, Wisconsin, and even from Europe.

While approximately ten subspecies provide the bulk of the hunting and recreation in the United States, there are some less important but nonetheless interesting subspecies that are confined to limited geographic areas. For example, there are four distinct and identifiable subspecies that inhabit the coastal islands off Georgia and South Carolina. These deer tend to be smaller than their mainland relatives. And although the barriers that separate them from the mainland are not great, the deer appear to have little appetite for negotiating the saltwater swamps and channels that separate them from the mainland, as evidenced by the distinctness of the subspecies that have evolved on these islands.

Of the major subspecies that inhabit the continent, it can be said that in general the northern species are larger than the southern ones. The largest are the Northern Woodland, Dakota, Northwest, and Columbian subspecies. The smallest of the United States subspecies is the Coues or Arizona whitetail. The smallest of the East Coast varieties is the Florida Key deer, which has been hard hit by man's invasion of its domain, by tropical storms, and by flooding. A brief description of the important subspecies of whitetail deer follows.

1. Virginia Whitetail Deer

    This is the deer mentioned in Barlowe's description of Roanoke Island in 1584. It is the deer that provided most of the fresh meat for the Jamestown settlers, and it is the deer that roamed the estates of Washington and Jefferson. It is large and bears heavy broad antlers, but it is not quite as large as its cousin to the north, the Northern Woodland Whitetail Deer.

2. Northern Woodland Whitetail Deer

    This is the deer of the northeastern United States. It is one of the largest of the whitetail deer subspecies, and it is found throughout New England, New York, New Jersey, Pennsylvania, Ohio, Illinois, Indiana, Wisconsin, Michigan, Minnesota, and parts of Canada. This deer seems to have adapted well to man's building and farming activities. It can be found in the woods, farmlands, and even on the fringes of suburbia. To the north, this deer has followed man's advance into the interior of Canada, living off farms and cutover forests along the way. Not only has this deer been observed pushing into new areas in Canada, but also it seems that he has been displacing the less aggressive mule deer from these ranges.

3. Dakota Whitetail Deer

    The Dakota is the largest of the subspecies of *Odocoileus virginianus* and has heavy antlers with a moderate spread and short tines. It is found at its largest in the plains and badlands of the Dakotas and in the heavily forested river valleys of this region.

4. Northwest Whitetail Deer

    Paler than the Northern Woodland variety this deer is similar in color to the Dakota deer, but is not quite as big. This is the deer of the northern Rocky Mountain region.

2-1 The whitetail deer has adapted well to man's infringement into his territory. Whitetails are found in farmlands and even in the fringes of suburbia over most of the United States. The deer in this photograph are of the rare Columbian subspecies. (Courtesy of the State of Washington Game Dept.)

5. Columbian Whitetail Deer

Another large subspecies of whitetail, the Columbian was nearly driven to extinction. The deer has been preserved in a small colony of about 500 animals on Puget Sound Island and another small colony of 300 animals on a state game preserve. There is some hope that this subspecies will be able to make a comeback.

6. Coues or Arizona Whitetail Deer

Also known as the fantail, the Coues is the smallest of the whitetail subspecies in the United States. This deer seems to have some mountain goat in his background, as it has shown a liking for the steepest mountain slopes in his range.

7. Texas Whitetail Deer

This is a large deer, much larger than the Coues to the west, but smaller than the Dakota to the north. The antlers of this variety tend to be slender with a large spread. In certain parts of Texas, local minerals give rise to large antlers and trophy racks.

8. Kansas Whitetail Deer

This is another of the subspecies that has been driven from most of its former range. It is unfortunate for the hunter that this should be so since this is a large animal with unusually thick antlers with a good spread.

9. Avery Island Whitetail Deer

This subspecies is found in the Louisiana bayou country

and in the marshes of southeastern Texas. It is smaller than the Texas deer but is nonetheless a good-sized animal. Its antlers are thinner than those of the Texas variety and curve sharply inward.

10, 11, 12, and 13. The Bulls Island, Hunting Island, Hilton Head Island, and Blackbeard Island Whitetail deer

These subspecies are found on the coastal islands off Georgia and South Carolina. They are all of medium size and of limited geographic interest.

14. Florida Coastal Whitetail Deer

This is a medium-sized deer found along the Gulf coasts of Alabama, Mississippi, and parts of Florida. It is similar to the Virginia whitetail, but on the average is somewhat smaller.

15. Florida Whitetail Deer

This is a large deer that inhabits most of the state of Florida. No doubt this is the subspecies that provided most of the hides for the eighteenth-century Florida export trade discussed in Chapter 1.

16. Florida Key Whitetail Deer

The Florida Key deer is the smallest whitetail found in the eastern United States. The deer was originally found over much of the southern Florida keys, but man's intrusion and violent hurricanes have reduced its numbers drastically.

Subspecies 17 through 30 are not of great interest to U.S. hunters and will not be discussed further here. The interested reader can find details in *The Deer of North America* by Walter P. Taylor.

Birth

The rut or mating period in the northern United States normally takes place in mid-November. After the roughly 199-day gestation period of the whitetail deer fawning occurs in late May or early June. The place of fawning is largely a matter of luck and depends on where the doe happens to be at the time. There is no apparent effort made by the doe to seek a particularly safe or secluded spot, and the nearest bit of cover at the time serves as her delivery room. There is quite a bit of variation in the weight of fawns at birth, depending on the mother's size, health, and diet. Male fawns average about seven-and-a-half pounds and female fawns about six pounds.

As anyone who has ever ventured forth in search of a buck can tell you, there seem to be ten does born for every buck. Surprisingly, however, there are actually more bucks born than does. The in utero ratio is about 117 males per 100 females. The male fawn mortality rate is a little higher than the mortality rate for female fawns, but even at five to seven months the ratio is still 106 males to 100 females. This is similar to humans and a number of other species of mammals where males account for 51 to 53 percent of all births.

The number of fawns to which a doe gives birth depends on the age of the doe and upon dietary conditions. Some does will breed as fawns at age six to seven months. Such does usually have single deliveries. Fertility increases with age until the doe is four-and-a-half years old, levels off till age seven and a half, and then decreases with old age. During the period of peak fertility, twins and triplets are common, and rare instances of quadruplets have been reported.

In the first few days after birth, the fawns are quite helpless and depend on camouflage for protection. A fawn will instinctively lie close to the ground and remain absolutely motionless when approached. Its spotted coat and small size make it very difficult to spot in the sunlight-dappled undergrowth where it seeks cover. During the first week or so of its existence, the fawn has little or no scent, making it doubly difficult for a would-be predator to find it.

Contributing to the scentless condition of the birthplace is the practice that the does make of eating their own afterbirth thus reducing the possibility that predators will be drawn to the area by its scent. It is also believed by biologists that the ingestion of the afterbirth may bring about the necessary hormonal changes in the doe to precipitate freshening.

I would strongly suggest that if you are in the woods during the birthing period that you do not disturb any young fawns you may find. The does do not lie with fawns but do come back periodically to feed them. Thus a fawn that may look quite deserted by its mother is probably being well cared for. Approaching close enough to the fawn to take a picture should do no harm, but do not pick the animal up (which will only terrify it) and do not move it.

Growth

Whitetail deer grow rapidly. The most rapid skeletal growth ends by the time the deer is seven months old, and a dressed male from a good range may weigh seventy to eighty pounds at this age. A lesser spurt in skeletal growth occurs during the animal's second summer, and healthy one-and-a-half-year-old males may weigh as much as 170 pounds. There is a lot of overlapping of sizes between fawns and yearlings and males and females. Thus body size is a highly unreliable determinant of sex for the hunter. The weight of the buck you finally bag will be dependent to a great extent on where it is that you hunt. Bucks from Pennsylvania average 110 to 120 pounds dressed, whereas reports from Maine indicate an average weight of about 150 pounds. Occasionally a monster is taken, and the New York State Department of Environmental Conservation owns the head of a beauty that reportedly weighed 388 pounds when it was shot in 1890. In Nebraska, the whitetails weigh more on the average than the mule deer!

Hunters who know the hog-dressed weight (heart, liver, and other viscera removed) of their deer often ask how much edible venison they can expect to get from their catch. The relationship between live weight, hog-dressed weight, and edible meat is shown in Figure 2–2. This figure gives average values for healthy animals shot in the fall of the year and is applicable to both bucks and does. The following examples illustrate the use of this chart.

2–2

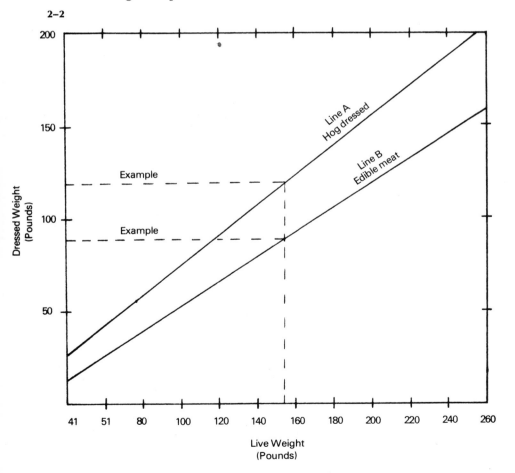

Assume the hunter knows that his hog-dressed deer weighs 120 pounds. He locates the 120-pound weight on the left scale of Figure 2–2, draws a horizontal line over till it intersects line A, and then draws a vertical line down to the bottom scale and reads the live weight as 156 pounds. From the point where his vertical line crossed line B, he draws another horizontal line back to the left scale and reads the amount of edible meat as eighty-four pounds. Results: hog-dressed weight, 120 pounds; live weight, 156 pounds; edible meat, 84 pounds. There will, of course, be some variation in these figures from deer to deer depending on range conditions, the animal's state of health, and the time of day, which will determine the fullness of the deer's paunch. Edible meat figures vary since some hunters use such parts as neck and ribs and some do not. Furthermore, less experienced hunters are likely to ruin more meat through poor bullet placement or because they need more than one shot to bring down their game. In any event, estimates from Figure 2–2 will probably be accurate to plus or minus five pounds. The heart and liver can be estimated as seven pounds for a 200-pound hog-dressed deer, three-and-a-half pounds for an 80-pound hog-dressed deer, and proportionally for anything in-between.

Antlers

Near and dear to the heart of every whitetail deer hunter is the subject of antlers. Even when the main motivation for the hunt is collecting venison, there is pride taken in the bagging of a bragging-size set of antlers.

Antler growth in the northern climates begins in April or May. The exact mechanism of growth stimulation is not known, but it is thought to be associated with increased pituitary activity and the secretion of a hormone called testosterone. These changes in hormone production have been linked by various authorities to changes in temperature, changed number of daylight hours, and changes in diet associated with the growth of the new spring vegetation. The antlers grow from the pedicles, the two skin-covered knobs on the skull. The antlers grow out from the pedicles as calcium is deposited to form the antlers. The skin that covers the pedicles grows along with the developing antler and keeps it completely covered until growth is completed. This covering of skin, which is called velvet, is rich in blood vessels and it supplies to the antler from the outside the nutrients and minerals necessary for the antler's development. The velvet is so full of blood vessels that it is actually quite warm to the touch. During the period of growth, the antlers are tender and easily injured. The bucks are well aware

2-3 Until late summer, the buck's new antlers are covered with velvet. The velvet is easily injured and contains the numerous blood vessels that nourish the growing antlers. (Courtesy of Tennessee Wildlife Resources Agency)

of this, and take great pains to avoid bumping their sprouting head ornaments.

The antlers become hard and the velvet is shed in September. The shedding of the velvet is brought on by an outward growth from the base of the antlers that effectively cuts off the blood supply to the velvet. The peeling velvet seems to cause the buck some annoyance and he sets about rubbing it off with considerable industry once it starts to shed. Some deer will rub off the velvet completely in the course of a day or two, while others may take weeks. Young whippy saplings are favorite targets for the bucks as they rub off their velvet, and the September woods are full of small trees with one or two foot sections of bark worn away by some buck's persistent rubbing.

A buck will continue to polish his newly developed weapons for some time after the velvet is gone. The rut is approaching, the air is getting crisp, and he begins to feel a certain restlessness. Besides, thin springy trees make good sparring partners. The result of all this activity is a set of polished antlers that may range from near white to a chocolaty brown. The color is determined primarily by the relative number of dried-out blood cells in the outer layers of the antlers. This in turn is regulated by range conditions, diet, and the general well-being of the animal. Other conditions that influence antler color are amount of rubbing, juices from plants upon which the antlers are rubbed, and exposure to sunlight. Once the rut is over, the buck sheds his antlers. Typically, this occurs between December and February. The shed antlers are occasionally found by hikers, campers, or hunters who stumble across them before they can be consumed by rodents.

A large, fully developed set of whitetail deer antlers is a thing of symmetric beauty. The whitetail's antlers develop long graceful curving main beams with each point growing out from the main beam. This growth pattern makes the whitetail easily distinguishable from the mule deer or the blacktail, whose antlers grow in a pattern of successive forks. The size of the antlers from specimen to specimen varies tremendously even within a given range. There is, however, a general trend toward increasing beam diameter with age. For typical New York State deer ranging in age from one-and-a-half to seven-and-a-half years, beam diameters range from .68 inches to 1.4 inches, with a slight decrease for older deer. But these figures depend strongly on range conditions. Again citing New York as an example, average beam diameters for deer from the heavily overpopulated Central Adirondack region are .63 inches, .87 inches, and 1.02 inches for one-and-a-half, two-and-a-half, and three-and-a-half-year-olds respectively. In the richer ranges of the western part of the state, the corresponding figures are .75 inches, .98 inches, and 1.1 inches. Similar remarks apply to the number of points in the rack. Virtually all buck fawns (about six or seven months old) have nubbins or buttons in their first fall and are commonly referred to by hunters as "button bucks." Most hunters believe that the following year, when the buck is one-and-a-half years old, he will have a set of "legal" three-inch spikes. However, studies in New York show that this is not necessarily the case. Specimens taken from the Central Adirondacks after an average or severe winter show that 50 percent of the one-and-a-half-year-old bucks will have antlers less than the three-inch New York legal minimum length. In addition, 15 percent of the two-and-a-half-year-olds and five percent of the three-and-a-half-year-olds will also have antlers less than three inches long!

Hunters often use the rule of thumb that a one-and-a-half-year-old buck will be a spikehorn, a two-and-a-half-year-old a fork-horn (four points), and a three-and-a-half-year-old will have six or more points. Under some range conditions this rule may have some rough correlation with reality. However, as indicated by the previous New York examples, antlers should not be used as a guide, even as a rough guide, in determination of a deer's age. Another study shows that a buck fawn, given all he wants of a balanced diet in his first winter, will weigh from 135 to 180 pounds when he is one-and-a-half years old and that he will have six- to eight-point antlers with beam lengths of twelve to fifteen inches. While it is true that most natural environments do not provide such a nutritious diet, a recently published study by the Michigan Department of Natural Resources shows that in game management Region III, the southern thirty-five counties of the state, the average point count for all one-and-a-half-year-old bucks taken over a seven-year period was 5.8 points and the average weight was 128.5 pounds hog-dressed. These figures certainly come close to the ideal laboratory results mentioned above, and show what proper herd management and good range can accomplish. So if you want to know what your chances are of bagging a good-size rack, I suggest that you check with the conservation department or the fish and game agency since conditions vary considerably even within a state.

2–4 This Tennessee buck is working on a bragging-size set of nontypical antlers! (Courtesy of Tennessee Wildlife Resources Agency)

In view of the tenderness of the developing antlers, it is not surprising that injury to the velvet-covered antlers is fairly common. Such injury often results in a set of "nontypical" antlers that may have only a minor irregularity on one side or may have gnarled misshapen growths with two or more main beams on each side. Besides injuries to the antler itself, some studies have related nontypical antler development to injuries to other parts of the deer's body. For example, an injury to the right rear leg may cause a malformation of the right antler. It is not known at present whether the antler malformation in such cases is transmitted sympathetically through the nervous system or whether it is the result of such purely mechanical factors as injury to the antler as the deer continually turns his head to lick his wound.

Although antlers are normally confined to bucks, hormonal imbalance has been known to cause antler development in does. The following article appeared in the *North Virginia Daily* under the headline "Rockland Hunter Bags Antlered Doe."

> When Gordon E. Smith of Rockland bagged a five-point deer on Thanksgiving morning he had no idea he had felled a rarity of the animal world.
>
> Smith's antlered deer turned out to be a doe with antlers still in velvet. According to James Simpson, game warden in Warren County, this is a rare specimen and the first he has ever seen in his lifetime.
>
> Smith said he spotted the deer from the upper porch of his home at dawn Thursday and felled it from there. On investigation he found it was actually a doe.
>
> At the Shell Service Station in Front Royal where he took the deer to be checked authorities were mystified as to how to record it and sent Smith to the game warden. Simpson said he checked the kill as an "antlered deer". . . .
>
> Smith said his kill weighed 105 pounds dressed and although the rack is not particularly impressive he is having the head mounted because of its uniqueness.
>
> Simpson said no charges were filed against Smith since he complied with regulations and killed a deer with antlers visible above the hair of the head.

Trophies

Trophy hunters have some rules of thumb that they utilize to estimate beforehand whether or not a trophy is of roughly record book proportions. Estimates on whitetail deer are particularly difficult to make since the hunter often gets no more than a furtive glance at a partially obscured rack. This is in contrast to such open-ground game as antelope and goats, which are often observed through a scope for some time. The rule that trophy hunters use on old

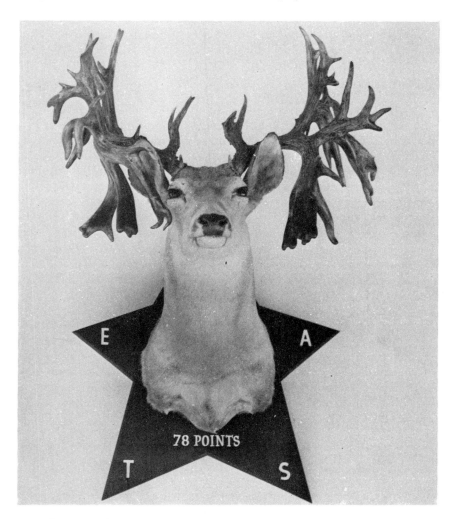

2–5 This incredible rack is currently the world record, nontypical whitetail deer trophy. It has seventy-eight points or protuberances and scores 286 points on the Boone and Crockett Club's scoring system. (Courtesy Lone Star Brewing Company)

whitey is that if the beam spread at its widest is as wide as the animal's body, he's a big one. Obviously this rule is usable only if the deer is viewed from the front or back. From the side, if the antlers appear to be roughly as high as the distance from the deer's brisket (breastbone) to his chin in normal standing position, he's another big one.

Whether or not your trophy makes it into the record books is determined by the folks at the Boone and Crockett Club and the National Rifle Association. Since 1974, the Boone and Crockett Club and the NRA have been the cosponsors of the North American Big Game Awards Program under which the trophies are scored and tabulated. Throughout the remainder of this book, I will refer to the scoring and tabulating system as the Boone and Crockett system or the Boone and Crockett records simply because this is the name by which the program is known to most hunters.

The Boone and Crockett Club was organized in 1887 under the leadership of Teddy Roosevelt and consisted of a group of outdoorsmen interested in conservation and trophy hunting. Among its other activities, the club compiles a list of trophy heads of various types of North American big game. In 1950, a standardized method of trophy measurement and scoring was established, and with little modification this system is still in use. For whitetail deer, the Boone and Crockett system recognizes four categories of entries. These categories are typical whitetail deer, nontypical whitetail deer, typical Coues deer, and nontypical Coues deer. The scoring system awards points for beam length, beam diameter, spread, number of points, and lengths of points. The system also penalizes typical racks for asymmetry between the right and left antlers. For example, if one beam had more points than the other, or if the points on the two beams were of different lengths, the score would suffer.

The measurements used to qualify a trophy for inclusion in the Boone and Crockett records must be made by one of a number of recognized game specialists and taxidermists, and at least sixty days must elapse after the kill before the measurements can be taken. The Club has established the following minimum scores for recognition of a trophy and inclusion in the records:

Whitetail deer, typical	170
Whitetail deer, nontypical	195
Coues deer, typical	110
Coues deer, nontypical	120

Where should one go to find a trophy head if he has the time, the money, and the inclination to leave his own back yard to

**Current Boone and Crockett Club World Record
Whitetail Deer Trophies**

TYPICAL ANTLERS

Rank	Score	Locality killed	Date
1	206⅝	Sandstone, Minnesota	?
2	205	Randolph Co., Missouri	1971
3	204½	Peoria Co., Illinois	1965
4	202	Funkley, Minnesota	1918
5	200⅞	Nemaha Co., Kansas	1974
6	200⅜	Clinton Co., Indiana	1974
7	199½	Clark Co., Missouri	1969

NONTYPICAL ANTLERS

1	286	Brady, Texas	1892
2	282⅝	Clay Co., Iowa	1973
3	277⅜	Hall Co., Nebraska	1962
4	272	Junction, Texas	1925
5	269⅛	Norman Co., Minnesota	1974
6	261¾	Holmes Co., Ohio	1975
7	261½	Pike Co., Ohio	1971

engage in the frustrating search for a trophy deer? Traditionally, the biggest racks come from such northern states as Maine and Minnesota. In recent years, due to hunting pressure and changes in range quality, the big rack areas seem to have shifted. The big trophies now seem to come from southern Canada, especially Saskatchewan, Manitoba, and Alberta. But I have a sneaky suspicion that the new number one head, if one ever comes along to displace the 206⅝-point monster presently leading the Boone and Crockett list, will come from America's corn belt. Somewhere in a cottonwood stand, along a sleepy river bottom in the corn country of Iowa, Nebraska, or thereabouts, lurks a buck so big that he would give Dan'l Boone himself buck fever. His rack is so big he looks like he has poplar trees growing out of his head. He's about four-and-a-half years old now, is corn fed, weighs over 300 pounds on the hoof, and was supporting eight points when he was just a yearling. When some lucky hunter topples this monster, the Boone and Crockett lists will have a new champ.

    The Boone and Crockett records include any head taken by legal means in a fair chase. Thus the records include trophies taken with bow and arrow as well as those taken with a gun. This places the archers at a disadvantage since their hunting technique is more difficult and demanding. To remedy this situation, a group of archers organized the Pope and Young Club in the state of Washington in 1963. This club maintains records of game taken with bow and

2–6 This symmetric beauty is the current world record typical whitetail deer trophy. The antlers have ten points (five on each side), and the main beams are each 30 inches long. The deer was killed in the vicinity of Sandstone, Minnesota, and it scores 206 5/8 on the Boone and Crockett Club's scoring system. (Courtesy of Charles T. Arnold)

arrow and the club uses a scoring system similar to Boone and Crockett's. Interestingly enough, many of the Pope and Young records rank high on the Boone and Crockett list.

Age

Antler development is a poor indicator of a deer's age. Even if it were accurate, the technique would be applicable only to bucks. The most accurate and reliable age indicator that biologists have found is the degree of development and wear of the deer's teeth. A deer with fully developed dentition has a total of thirty-two teeth. In the lower jaw it has six incisors, two canines, six premolars, and six molars. The upper jaw contains six premolars and six molars. This tooth distribution comes as a surprise to many hunters who take the time to examine their deer's teeth because they find that the deer has front teeth on the bottom jaw, but no opposing front teeth on the upper jaw. Instead, there is a tough fleshy pad in the upper jaw opposite the lower jaw incisors. The deer presses the vegetation it is trying to sever against this pad with its lower incisors and the result is the familiar jagged cut found on deer browse.

Up to the age of seventeen or eighteen months, the deer's age can be determined quite accurately by simply determining which teeth are present in the jaw since the last new teeth come in at about seventeen months. After seventeen months, age can most accurately be determined by checking the amount of wear on the teeth. While the amount of tooth wear at a given age will vary slightly from place to place depending on range and soil conditions, this method of age determination has proved to be quite accurate. Many state game departments have compiled collections of known-age jaws and from these jaws developed an age-determination system for local deer. You can probably obtain a chart from your local game department that can be used to get an idea of your deer's age. But if you want an accurate determination, let an expert do it for you since the distinctions between different degrees of wear are often subtle.

Pelage

Pelage is a game biologist's word for what hunters call the deer's coat, hair, or fur. The whitetail deer fawn is born with a complete covering of light tawny hair that differs from the adults' coat most markedly in that the fawn's coat has several irregular rows of pure white spots running the length of the body on either side of the spine. This spotted coat gives the fawn a dappled appearance and allows it to blend in well with the sunspotted undergrowth where it spends its first weeks. It keeps its baby coat for three or four months after which time it goes through its first molt or change of coat.

2–7 A fawn's dappled coat is an example of protective coloration and it helps the young animal blend in with the sun-spotted undergrowth where he spends his first few weeks. The fawn will keep this spotted coat for three or four months at which time he will undergo his first molt. (Courtesy Virginia Commission of Game and Inland Fisheries. L.G. Kesteloo)

Whitetail deer go through a molt twice each year. The first molt, which occurs in the spring, begins in March in the southern latitudes and as late as early June in northern climates. In all latitudes this molt is over by about the third week in June, at which time the deer has completed the changeover to its summer dress. The summer dress is reddish brown, and the hairs are shorter and of lesser diameter allowing for better air circulation. This coat is a short-term garment intended for summer comfort only, and the animal begins to shed it in August or early September.

The winter coat, which is fully donned in most areas by the end of September, is the whitetail deer's courting finery. It is a heavier, coarser coat than the light summer one, and it is dark brown with black tips on the hair that give the coat a blue-gray tint at times. This thick winter coat gives the deer the insulation it needs to get through the long, cold, windy winter nights. The insulation provided by the coat is so good that snow falling on a sleeping deer will often accumulate without melting, and the snow beneath a bedded deer will often be compressed but show little sign of melting.

There are abnormal coat colorings in whitetail deer that cause great excitement among hunters. Melanism, the growth of a black coat, is rare and has been reported, although I am aware of no truly melanistic coats that have been preserved. Mottled or piebald deer are much more common. In the Northeast, about one piebald

2–8 Mottled or piebald deer are not considered to be great rarities. In the Northeast, about one deer in every 5,000 killed is piebald. (Courtesy Virginia Commission of Game and Inland Fisheries. L.G. Kesteloo)

deer in 5,000 is reported each hunting season. These deer vary from predominantly brown specimens with white spots to predominantly white deer with various blotchy brown or black spots. In addition, about one in 5,000 is observed to have rows of irregular light-brown spots running down either side of the spine in a manner reminiscent of the fawn's spots. These spots may be shadows from the past, and it is thought that possibly they resemble the color pattern on the coat of one of the whitetail's primeval ancestors.

The color abnormality that most stirs the hunter's imagination with visions of a rare and beautiful trophy is the all-white variety. Occasionally one hears reports of an albino specimen. A true albino is devoid of pigmentation, has pink eyes and skin, and like the melanistic variety is quite rare. However, in recent years there has been an increasing number of reports of all-white nonalbino deer. Such deer have been reported in several places in New York, Vermont, and Virginia, and they have normal pigmentation except for the white hair. In fact, the taxidermist who mounts my deer for me in Virginia has two specimens hanging on his wall. The coat on these deer is not blotchy. It is not off-white. It is brilliant, all-over-like-new-fallen-snow white.

The largest group of all-white deer of which I am aware is the herd at the Seneca Army Depot in the Finger Lakes region of New York. The herd at the depot consists of some 200 to 300 of these striking creatures. The white deer run, mix, and breed interchangeably with their brown brethren. In matings between the two color strains, the offspring are either brown or white, never mixed. Two white parents have been known to give birth to normally colored brown progeny. Besides having white coats, the white deer have another distinguishing characteristic. Their antlers tend to be nontypical by normal deer standards because their antlers are often palmated and resemble somewhat the antlers of a young moose.

Biologists believe that the white coloration is the result of a genuine genetic mutation and they further believe that the white mutant may be the dominant gene in view of the way the number of whites has grown since they were first observed at Seneca in 1957. If this is the case, we may one day find these deer transplanted and white herds started in other states.

3

The Whitetail's Habits and Senses

If you are fishing for trout, you don't fish in warm-water swamps; and if you are looking for large-mouth bass, you can forget about crystal-clear, cold, spring-fed mountain streams. Likewise, if you propose to bag a buck, you would be well advised to know as much as you can about the animal's habits and range. After all, it's his druthers and not yours that determine where you should look for him.

Annual Patterns of Movement

Whitetail deer are not migratory in the true sense of the word. The biggest annual relocation that most whitetail undertake is the relatively minor shift from their summer to winter ranges and back again. These shifts rarely involve moves of more than a few miles and usually are much less than that. Extensive studies show that the average whitetail deer lives and dies within a mile of its birthplace. The home-range instinct is so deeply rooted in the animal that if it is driven off its range by hunting pressure, weather conditions, or other factors, it will return to its original range as soon as possible. Furthermore, it is driven off its range only with difficulty. Even in the face of heavy hunting pressure, a deer will usually circle back past the hunters, hide, or wait till nightfall to get back to the mountain ridge or conifer stand that it calls home. In the course of game studies, deer have been tagged and transported away from their home range. These studies, conducted in such diverse areas as New York, Michigan, and Texas, show that deer transported and released less than ten miles from home have a high probability of returning to their original range. Somewhere between ten and twenty miles there is a point at which the deer becomes so disoriented that it is no longer able to tell which way is home, and will simply settle down in the new area. The urge to stay on familiar ground is so strong that there are repeated reports that deer will starve to death rather than move to ranges with sufficient food a few miles away. This is not to say that deer cannot be displaced from their range. If they are heavily hunted and continually disturbed in their bedding areas, deer will shift to a more secluded spot.

The summer range of the whitetail includes almost all the land in those regions that it inhabits except for the very highest elevations. The deer are not commonly found at elevations above about 4,000 feet in the Northeast nor above about 7,000 feet in the West. However, some deer are found even at these elevations, and there is a school of hunters who believe in hunting these high ridges for trophy deer since the only critter found less frequently than deer at these heart-arresting elevations is the road-bound hunter.

In early summer, deer show a preference for areas along the shores of lakes and bogs. Here some of the first succulent green herbs burst forth into spring and into the mouths of the winter-starved herd. The deer dine on such delicacies as algae and water lilies and are often seen standing belly-deep in the water pursuing their favorite groceries.

While the location of the summer range is based largely on dietary considerations, such is not the case with the winter range. The winter range's selection is based on protection from the elements. In general, the deer come down to lower elevations to get away from cold winter winds. They seek out protected saddles and hollows. They look for slopes with southern exposures. These are the slopes that are occasionally snow free even in February and March. They look for frozen swamps with heavy growths of cedars or conifers. They look for places to herd together in communal areas called yards. And in some parts of the country, they are looking for areas in which to starve to death in numbers so great as to stagger the imagination.

Winter is hard on the whitetail deer. Over much of its range, from the East Coast to the West, the number of deer exceeds the carrying capacity of the range. As the snows get deeper and the nights get colder, food becomes harder to find. The first to go are the old and the sick. They are followed quickly by the young, who are unable to reach the higher browse and who have smaller bodies with less reserved fat. Writing in the October–November 1972, issue of *The Conservationist*, C. W. Severinghaus estimated that during the three severe winters of 1968 thru 1971, five out of every six fawns in the Adirondacks was a winter kill. Severinghaus recognizes two different snow depths that are critical to the whitetail herd — fifteen inches and twenty inches. At depths greater than fifteen inches, the fawns have trouble negotiating the snow and burn up a lot of energy if they try to do so. At depths greater than twenty inches, the adults have similar difficulties. Severinghaus feels that the deer will survive quite well if there are fewer than forty days with fifteen inches of snow accumulated. Similarly, if there are fewer than thirty days with twenty inches of snow, the deer should fare well. When the figures get to sixty days of fifteen-inch accumulation or fifty days with twenty inches of accumulation, serious losses can be expected.

Starvation in deer is a drawn-out and tragic end for the poor creatures. A deer normally consumes six to twelve pounds of browse each day and can survive for extended periods on as little as two or three pounds daily. The starvation process is literally a self-consumptive process. The deer first absorbs the fat stored under its skin. Once this is gone, its body resorts to the fat in the marrow of its bones. During this period the deer will do everything possible to conserve energy and body heat. It will sometimes lie in its bed for days at a time rather than consume energy by moving about. It will suffer from dehydration rather than eat snow and make its body use some of its precious heat to melt the snow in its mouth. Slowly its marrow turns from white to pink to red as the malnutrition worsens. Experts estimate that once a deer has lost between a third and half of its body weight, the point of no return has been passed. Deer in this condition brought in from the field have shown little interest in food and have died within a few weeks. It has been estimated that as many as 2 million deer of all types starve each year in this country. Most of this starvation occurs within a 100-day period. This means that on a typical cold night in February, upwards of 20,000 deer starve to death.

Daily Patterns of Movement

There is considerable disagreement among authorities on deer concerning daily movement patterns of the animal. Some claim that the whitetail deer is naturally a nocturnal animal. Other experts claim that in remote areas, where the deer are not disturbed by man, they are diurnal, and that when man invades their realm, the deer resort to movement by night to avoid him. Both groups seem to agree that the animal prefers to feed in the early morning and in the evening with a preference for the evening hours. I, however, think the deer is a seminocturnal-semidiurnal creature with variable eating and sleeping habits.

Trying to generalize on the daily life patterns of deer is further complicated by the whitetail deer's great individualism. When all the other deer are snoozing in the warm midday sunshine, there will invariably be one or two nonconformists who decide to get up and go for a snack. When most of the others head out into a rock-strewn field for lunch, some other individualists will head for the stream. Further complicating the situation is the strong influence that local conditions have on the deers' habits. Even though the deer might act in a certain way if they were not disturbed by man, the fact remains that in most places they are disturbed by man, the nature and timing of the disturbance varying from place to place. In spite of these uncertainties, I will attempt to describe a typical daily movement pattern for deer in, say, the month of August. I fully realize that some hunters will read this and say, "Whatta dummy! No deer in my neck of the woods moves like that!" To which I can only reply that one cannot learn everything he needs to know about deer hunting from a book, and there is no substitute for actually getting out and finding out how the deer move in your neck of the woods.

Our group of typical deer are bedded down in their night bedding area. The night beds are on the side of a pine-covered knoll and the deer have selected dry, level spots in the pine needles close to the trunks of the trees and under the cover of the overhanging boughs. The old doe is the first to rise. She takes a step or two, bends down and nudges a sleeping fawn with her nose. There is a flurry of gangling legs, white tail, and little white spots, and the fawn is on its feet. Nearby a second fawn gets up more slowly — back legs up first, then the front legs straighten out. Several trees away, a young buck gets up also. He is one of this doe's fawns of the previous year, and he still travels with the matriarchal family group. The doe and the buck stand there for a few minutes testing the air with their noses. They look this way and that and their ears seem to swivel in all directions listening for foreign noises. The doe

3-1 A doe and her fawn out for a morning stroll. (Courtesy of Ontario Ministry of Industry and Tourism)

is the first to start down the well-defined path to the pond that lies a few hundred yards down the hillside. She is followed closely by the two fawns and at a somewhat greater distance by the young buck who is still in velvet. The deer do not travel in strict single file, but meander back and forth off the trail browsing on some lichen here and some young leaves there. At the slightest sound the old doe freezes, her head pops up, and she stares intently in the direction of the noise. Convinced there is no danger, she takes a few more steps and continues her browsing.

By the time this family foursome gets to the pond, the sun is up and the morning mist is rising in eerie little streamers from the surface of the pond. The doe stops at the woodline, surveys the situation, and proceeds slowly to the edge of the pond. There she be-

3–2 Sometime during the course of a day's travels, a whitetail deer will pass by a stream or a local watering hole. A mature deer needs one or two quarts of water per day per hundred pounds of body weight. The deer can get this water either from vegetation or drinking, but vegetation alone is rarely enough. (Courtesy Virginia Commission of Game and Inland Fisheries.)

gins feeding on the tender shoots sprouting up along the edge of the pond. The young buck is more venturesome and wades freely out into the pond in search of water lilies.

The deer will continue to feed thus for about an hour. Whitetail deer are fond of water, and the buck and fawns may well take a short swim or two to escape the deer flies and for the sheer fun of swimming. About 8 A.M. the family group reassembles and moves slowly back up the hill to a field near the bedding ground. Here they will select daytime beds in the waist-high grass. No effort will be made to use the same beds as yesterday, and the deer will move several times in the course of the day.

At about 6 P.M. the doe will rise again and start moving toward the green grass along the lower edge of the field. She grazes as she goes and stops every few steps to look for signs of danger. The evening feeding period will last till slightly after dark, at which time the old doe will lead her charges back to their night beds on the pine-covered hill.

These behavior patterns, are, of course, highly variable. In the West, for example, deer will commonly bed down either very close to or right in their feeding areas. Hence daily movements are less pronounced. Whereas deer in the northern parts of the country look for warm, sunny areas to bed in, in the South and Southwest just the opposite is true. In the Gulf states, one would expect the deer to make their daytime beds in cool shady areas. In Texas and Arizona, gullies, arroyos, and shady canyon walls are favorite daytime retreats. In addition to these regional differences, the deer will vary their behavior in response to hunting pressure and other activities of man. More night feeding will be resorted to if the deer are being heavily pursued and disturbed during the day.

Certain generalizations of value to the hunter can, nonetheless, be made. The deer tend to move about in the early morning as they move from their night beds to the morning feeding areas. They will usually bed down till the afternoon and begin moving some time between 3 P.M. and 5 P.M. They will stay abroad until some time between 9 P.M. and 1 A.M., again depending on local conditions. The hunting techniques designed to capitalize on these recurrent behavior patterns are the techniques most likely to succeed.

Senses and Physical Capabilities

Whitetail deer have extremely sensitive senses of hearing, smell, and sight; and an old buck will use these senses to his utmost to insure that his venerable old hide doesn't spring any fatal leaks during hunting season. The biggest advantage that a deer has over you in the woods is its sense of smell. Under proper wind conditions, a deer can smell you as far as half a mile away. And deer place great reliance on this sense. So sure are they of their sense of smell, that they expend most of their looking and listening effort in the downwind direction since this is the direction from which they can't smell danger.

Deer come equipped with two dishpan-size ears that can hear a mosquito burp at 300 yards. To make these imposing eavesdropping devices even more effective, the ears come with independent suspension as standard equipment, enabling the animal to point one ear in one direction and the other ear in another direction. Three-hundred-and-sixty-degree protection as it were.

Deer are often accused of having mediocre to poor eyesight. In my experience this has not been the case. It is true that deer are color blind. When one sees the entire world in shades of gray, it is difficult to pick objects out—unless they move. The slightest bit of strange movement will immediately catch a deer's attention. As soon as a deer spots something that it thinks is suspicious, it will lock both ears in on the object and stare at it until convinced that it is harmless. I recall an incident that occurred while bowhunting in Virginia. I had seen a group of deer walk past my position at a distance of about 100 yards. Convinced they were not going to come any closer, I decided to play Natty Bumppo and try to sneak up on them. At a distance of about forty yards someone reached out and placed a treacherous dry twig under my foot just as I was stepping forward. Snap! As if on command, three heads popped up; and I had the undivided attention of three noses, six ears, and six big brown eyes. Feeling somewhat self-conscious at all this attention, I froze in place with a big grin that was meant to demonstrate friendly intent. The deer didn't seem convinced, and I began to feel like Davy Crockett trying to grin down a "bar." But I was determined to remain motionless for as long as necessary — except for one little thing. It never occurred to me that deer might think it impolite to blink under such circumstances. So I went ahead and blinked. And those deer lit out like there was a pack of blue tick hounds on their trail. I figure that if that little blink could cause all that panic at forty yards, their eyesight can't be too bad.

3–3 This doe is alerted to the presence of danger. She will remain thus alerted until her concern is alleviated and her curiosity is satisfied. (Courtesy of the State of Washington Game Dept.)

Just because deer are color blind, don't get the impression that they are totally insensitive to color. There is some reason to believe that deer may be able to detect the new blaze-orange and psychedelic-iridescent plastic geegaws that have come into vogue recently for hunter protection. Of course, these colors are so loud that the deer may be hearing them and not seeing them.

In view of the acuity of the deer's senses, it is not surprising that he usually spots you long before you spot him.

When it comes to mobility, the deer is well adapted to the terrain in which it lives. Long-forgotten ancestors of the deer had five toes on each foot, but the foot structure on today's deer is much modified. One of the toes has undergone complete evolutionary atrophy, and no external evidence of it remains. The first and fourth toes have receded and remain only as small dewclaws. The second and third toes have developed, and the toenails of these toes are the tough, resilient hooves of the animal. These hooves give the deer good traction in most terrains and, in combination with its light frame and strong, springy muscles, an overland capability that is truly incredible. Deer can sustain speeds of twenty-five miles per hour for extended periods. They have been clocked in bursts from thirty-five to forty miles per hour. Even in rough terrain they do not have to slow down appreciably because of their considerable jumping ability. An adult whitetail deer can jump from twenty-five to thirty feet with ease in a broad jump and can clear obstacles eight to nine feet high with no difficulty. As for agility, it can make a 180° change in direction so fast that it looks like an instant head-for-tail transplant.

There are certain circumstances, though, where the whitetail deer's hoof structure is its undoing. On slick ice, the deer is helpless. Its hooves give it little or no traction, it slips, falls, and is often unable to get up. Deer scared onto ice by hunters or dogs will sometimes die there if not found and rescued. They exhaust themselves in the struggle to get up and often break their limbs in their efforts. The American Indian was aware of this liability of the deer and would drive the animal out onto frozen lakes where it was easy prey. Another shortcoming of the deer's hoof is that its small surface area causes the deer to sink into soft materials such as snow and muddy pond bottoms. Normally this is no more than a minor aggravation; but if the deer is weak or being pursued, it could be fatal.

Deer seem to like water, and the many instances of their being sighted in the water can be ascribed to swimming just for the fun of swimming. At times a dip in the local pond does serve a utilitarian purpose: it enables the deer to wash off the mud that he has picked up on his legs during shoreside browsing and provides a

3-4   Deer are fond of water and have been clocked at swimming speeds of 10 to 15 knots. (Courtesy Virginia Commission of Game and Inland Fisheries)

respite from the ever-present deer flies. Deer have been sighted three to four miles from land in both freshwater and saltwater and have been clocked at swimming speeds of ten to fifteen knots.

The Family Group, Herding, and the Rut

The whitetail deer fawn grows up in a matriarchal society. From the time it is born until it leaves its mother sometime between six and fifteen months of age, the mother provides guidance and companionship. It is a rare family group that contains a buck other than one of the doe's own progeny. One exception to this behavior pattern occurs during the rut, at which time the doe temporarily abandons her family and seeks the company of a buck. Some bucks will stay with a doe in estrus for from seven to ten days, at which time she is no longer receptive. Other bucks show no inclination to remain faithful and will service several does in the course of a day.

The rutting behavior of deer is important to hunters, since in many areas the rut and the hunting season coincide or overlap. The rut in the northern and central parts of the country occurs in mid-November, and somewhat later in the South. The dates of the rut are somewhat indefinite, particularly in the warm climates where mating has been observed for as long as six months.

But the peak of the rut occurs sometime in November in most parts of the country. As the air gets crisper and the days get shorter there stir inside the bucks feelings that have moved their male forebears since time immemorial. They exercise their shiny new antlers on saplings and their necks begin to swell. The dominant animals stake out territories of their own and try to lure receptive does. To this end they scrape the leaves and twigs away from a patch of ground adjacent to a major runway and urinate on the bare ground. The bucks then stir the resultant mud into a mess that is supposed to be irresistible to does. A buck will usually stake out several such areas and make the rounds from one to the other several times a day to see what libidinous lassie may have dropped by to see him since he last visited his carefully constructed courting place. Smaller bucks will stand by and watch these antics, hoping to catch some winsome doe in a receptive mood when the local lord of the manor isn't around or is engaged in other romantic pursuits. Should one of these onlookers decide to test the mettle of the local dominant buck, the two will square off against one another in a head-ramming duel that may last for an hour or more. The two bucks will back up from one another to a distance of about ten feet, lower their heads, and then charge. Upon contact they twist and snort and stamp the ground and raise a general commotion that can be heard for some distance. The battle, for all its apparent ferocity, is meant to serve one of nature's purposes and serious injury rarely results. The battle usually ends with the loser leaving the scene with rumpled dignity and the victor too tired to do anything about the nearby does that he may have won. Every year there are several reports of deer that have locked horns while fighting and were subsequently unable to disengage their antlers. These unfortunate animals are doomed to die a slow death of exhaustion and starvation in this Siamese position. Bucks consume tremendous amounts of energy during the rut and weight losses of 10 to 15 percent are not uncommon even in healthy animals.

The actual mating procedure is an interesting spectacle—and a spectacle it is. I recall a bow-hunting outing that I took on a warm November day in Orange County, New York. I was stalking along in my best bow-hunting fashion and was slowly approaching a ridge line hoping to pop over the top and surprise some unsuspecting fourteen-pointer on the other side. As I got close to the top, I could hear leaves rustling and twigs snapping on the other side of the tree-covered ridge. The closer I got to the ridge the louder the din became, and I was about ready to stop stalking and just pop over the ridge to see what was going on. Just as I was ready to peek over the ridge, a spikehorn buck popped over the ridge about fifty yards to my left front and with occasional glances back in the direction from which he came, he walked up the ridge line away from me. This was just too much! Fifty yards is outside of my bow shooting range, but I wasn't about to try to get closer to that spikehorn. I just had to have a little peek at what was going on over that hill. I crept over the ridge and saw on the other side a depression about fifty yards long and thirty yards wide with an occasional blown-down tree in the hollow. A six-point buck had staked the area out as his territory, and some little filly was leading him on a merry chase.

The deer had worn out a large oval path around the perimeter of the depression. The buck would chase his lady friend frantically around the loop for two or three laps. Then, as if in response to some unseen signal, the two would come to a sudden halt and freeze. They would stare at one another for ten or fifteen seconds, and the doe would take off in the other direction and around and around they would go. The circuit they were running crossed some of the blown-down trees, and the pair would leap effortlessly over these obstacles, some of which were four feet off the ground. I watched this crazy undertaking for about half an hour, during which time the buck never did catch up with his lady friend.

Once the rage of the rut is spent, the does rejoin their little family groups and the bucks resume their somewhat more solitary existence. If yarding is not necessary during the winter, this condition continues on into the spring when the deer descend en masse onto the first grazing area that provides spring food. This is the time of year that herds of from twenty-five to fifty deer are often seen in fields and meadows—and herds of as many as 400 have been reported. The period of spring gregariousness ends in late May as the birthing period arrives and the does become bound to the spot of ground where their temporarily immobile fawns were born. Once the fawns are up and about, whitetail society reverts back to a matriarchy centered on the small family group. At this time the bucks begin to regrow the antlers they lost the previous winter, and the cycle of life begins anew.

Dietary Preferences

A knowledge of the deer's diet and dietary preferences is important to the hunter since it helps him locate likely feeding areas and the routes to and from these areas. The whitetail deer is a browser as opposed to a grazer. This means that deer tend to eat such foods as tender young growth on trees and shrubs and to avoid or minimize their intake of grasses. In addition to new growth, deer are very fond of beechnuts, acorns, and chestnuts. (These nuts are commonly referred to collectively as "mast.")

The diet of deer varies greatly across the country, and it has been documented that, nationwide, deer feed on over 600 species of plants, shrubs, and trees. In addition to the regional differences, diet is also strongly dependent on time of year. The acorns that are so abundant in some areas during the fall are hard to find during spring and summer and are replaced in the diet at these times by other foods. The most important and most readily consumed whitetail deer foods, by area of the country, are as follows.

NORTHEAST	
Apple (especially fruit)	Honeysuckle
Ash	Maple (all types)
Basswood	Oak
Birch	Sumac
Dogwood	White cedar
Highbush cranberry	Wild raisin
Witch hobble	

SOUTHEAST	
Black gum	Maple
Blueberry	Sumac
Cedar	Supplejack
Dogwood	Sweet gum
Grape	Titi
Greenbriar	White bay
White oak	

SOUTHWEST	
Cedar	Mesquite
Doveweed	Oak
Forestiera	Persimmon
Fringe tree	Prickly pear
Grape	Winged elm
Hackberry	Yellow jasmine

NORTHWEST	
Bearberry	Juniper
Black moss	Poplar
Buckbrush	Shadbush
Chokecherry	Sumac
Dogwood	Twinflower
Fungi	Western yellow fir
Grape	Yucca

As range conditions deteriorate, or as snow gets deeper, deer will resort to less desirable foods. These less desirable foods are not listed above since they include virtually any edible plant matter. In fact, deer have been known to starve with their bellies full of dead, dried-out twigs and other nutritionally useless matter.

Part Two

The
Weapons

4

Marksmanship

It may appear to be putting the cart before the horse to begin a section on weapons and weapon selection with a discussion of marksmanship, but many of the decisions that the hunter must make concerning choice of caliber, type of action, and type of sights are greatly facilitated if he has a good grasp of what marksmanship is all about and has set for himself in advance some standards of marksmanship.

When the time comes that I have followed my last set of deer tracks through the snow, squeezed off my last round, and I'm heading for the Happy Hunting Ground (where, I'm assured, all the racks are at least eight-pointers), it will probably not be said of me that I have very many whitetail deer trophies high on the Boone and Crockett list. I doubt that I will be remembered as the greatest tracker that ever lived. And if the past is any indication of the future, the U. S. Olympic Committee is not likely to expend much effort between now and my passing trying to get me on any of their marksmanship teams. But there is one thing for which I would like to be remembered—as a hunter who invariably dropped his game with a single shot. I can think of no greater accolade that one can accord a serious hunter.

One-shot kills don't require spectacular marksmanship—just good marksmanship. What one-shot kills do require is a lot of discipline. The hunter has to know what he can and can't hit, and he must discipline himself to shoot only at those targets that he is quite certain he can hit with a single, well-placed, lethal shot. He must discipline himself so well that he is not tempted after a long and frustrating no-shot day to shoot at marginal targets.

At this point you might well ask, What's so critical about the first shot? Isn't a kill on the second or third shot nearly as good? Yes, a kill on the second or third shot is nearly as good. But my experience has been that if the average hunter doesn't kill, or at least incapacitate, the game on his first shot, he doesn't do it on the second or third shot either. After the first shot the hunter is recovering from the recoil and blast. His adrenaline is flowing. And the target presented for the second and third shots is usually not nearly as good as for the first.

There are many advantages to one-shot kills. The most obvious of these is humanitarian. A hunter who usually takes two or three shots to get his deer probably leaves a lot of cripples behind him in a hunting lifetime. Under many hunting conditions there is no opportunity for a second or third shot, just the first. Another reason for shot discipline is hunter safety. Environmental groups tell us that lead in the air in molecular size from automobile exhausts is a health hazard. They ain't seen nuthin' till they've seen 150-grain chunks of lead in the air zinging along at 1,500 to 3,000 feet per second. An encounter with a piece of lead like that could ruin your whole day.

Another reason for good shot placement is conservation of venison. It's no great trick to place two or three shots into a deer and find that you have ruined a third or more of your best roasts and steaks. The hunter should also take some personal pride in dropping his game with one shot. It's similar to the distinction between taking 100 swings with an ax to fell a tree and taking only 40 swings. The net result may look somewhat similar, but the experienced lumberjack takes pride in his expertise in his craft. So should the hunter.

Do not conclude from the foregoing that I condemn such less-potent weapons as bows and arrows or such techniques as snap-shooting. I certainly do not. If you can use these weapons and techniques effectively and consistently get kills, I highly recommend them. But the type of weapon to be used and the method of employing it are very personal matters. Some hunters are simply better marksmen than others. I know some hunters who couldn't consistently drop deer at fifty yards using a 105-mm howitzer loaded with grapeshot. On the other hand, rumor has it that there's an old trapper outside of Caribou, Maine, who sets a sharp ax standing upright in the ground by his favorite deer trail. He fires on the sharp edge of the blade, splits the bullet, and gets two deer with every shot to conserve bullets.

This brings up the question of what percentage of the deer that you fire at should you bring down. This is a difficult question and the answer ultimately depends on personal standards of sportsmanship. If you have bagged three deer in the last three seasons, but fired at six, I personally think that's much too low a percentage of kills. That means there is a good chance that you left three cripples in the woods in three years. I think that a responsible hunter should bag a minimum of 90 percent to 95 percent of the deer at which he fires.

Shot Placement

In achieving one-shot kills, accurate shot placement is of central importance. How accurate is accurate? The maximum range at which you can keep your shots in a twelve-inch circle is the maximum range at which you should be taking broadside shots at whitetail deer. This maximum range depends on, among other things, the hunter's position. A typical rifle hunter may find, for example, that his maximum ranges are 350 yards prone, 200 yards sitting, and 100 yards offhand (standing). These distances are an individual matter, and you must determine them beforehand on a rifle range. If the shot is not broadside, but an angling, front, or rear shot, the target area is much smaller (about a six-inch circle) and all ranges must be cut in half. Figure 4–1 shows the vital areas for shot placement on a deer. In discussions of shot placement in books and magazines, one often sees strangely shaped pears, ovals, and strips that supposedly represent the deer's vital areas drawn on an outline of the deer. These figures are, in my humble opinion, about as useful as vitamin C in rat poison. What the once-a-year hunter needs is an aiming point—a place to hold his crosshairs while he squeezes the trigger. Points of aim are what are shown in Figure 4–1. The broadside figure (a) shows a twelve-inch bull's-eye, and the front, rear, and quartering figures (b, c, and d) show six-inch circles. The point of aim should be the center of these circles. The last figure (e) shows two broadside shots that can be used if you are close enough to be sure of your shot. The neck shot is a favorite of some hunters:

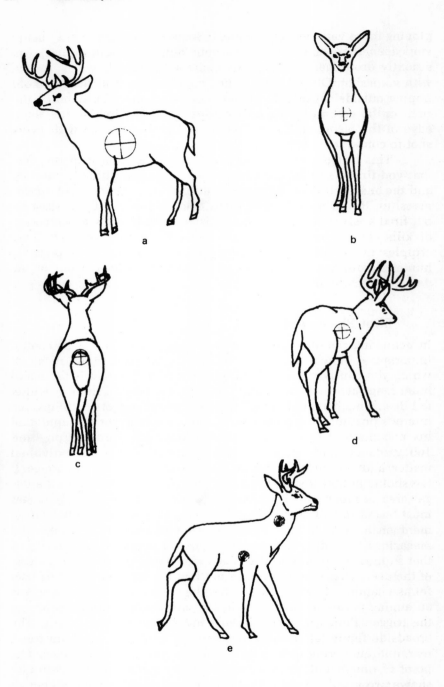

4–1   Shot Placement

it ruins little meat, and properly executed it results in a neatly dropped deer. A shot in the back half of the neck will either break the spine or at least disrupt the central nervous system. A shot in the front half will sever the windpipe and possibly the jugular vein. It might seem that a deer hit in the latter area could run some distance, but the area is so sensitive and full of nerve endings that a shot placed in the forward half of the neck almost invariably results in a deer that drops on the spot. A little concentrated effort, though, can turn the neck shot into a miss. My broadside favorite is the lung/heart shot shown in Figure 4–1e. The bullet goes in the rib cage on one side, penetrates, possibly comes out the rib cage on the other side, and destroys little edible meat en route. After being so hit, a deer will usually travel a total of about eighteen inches — straight down.

The anal shot shown in the figure can be used if necessary, but it is not one that I highly recommend. The bullet must travel through a lot of paunch to get to the vital organs, and if it doesn't make it you will have a cripple on your hands. I would not attempt this shot with a weapon less powerful than a 300 Winchester Magnum, and I would never try it on a running deer.

Practice

I highly recommend marksmanship practice. Most hunters don't do enough of it. The reasons are many: laziness, expense, inconvenience, and others. But if you don't pour a box of lead through your blunderbuss each year (cost, about nine dollars) you are being very negligent. And certain specialized types of shooting, such as snapshooting, take a lot more than one box (twenty rounds) of practice to maintain proficiency.

I have done very little competitive shooting, and what I have done has all been small bore. All my big-bore shooting has been in the military service and limbering up for hunting seasons. Since I own a small arsenal of big-bore rifles and shotguns usable on deer, I would find it difficult to remember grouping patterns, bullet weights, sight adjustments, and other vital statistics from year to year if I did not write them down. Therefore, I have resorted to keeping a shooter's notebook. I have a separate section in the notebook for each of my guns. I take the notebook with me every time I go shooting and make notes in it on the performance of the gun and ammunition. I also note down the sight adjustment and either write down a description of the shot group or, better yet, cut the bull's-eye out of the target and tape it into the notebook. If I don't use that gun again for some time or forget what sight settings I want when I

DATE: OCT 17, 1973
PLACE: IZAAK WALTON PARK

The zero seems to have settled down after installation of new sights. Using the settings shown below, the group shown on the following target was fired at 100 yds.

WINDAGE

ELEVATION

4–2

change bullet weights, all I have to do is turn to the appropriate section of the notebook to refresh my memory.

And when I go on a hunting trip, I always take the notebook along with me (it's of surprisingly little value sitting at home in the bookcase). That way, if I'm sitting around the camp at night and decide to change from 150-grain to 180-grain bullets, I know what my sight settings should be and where the bullet will impact.

What type of practicing should you do? Practice the type of shots that you plan to take. If you like to trail watch, prone and sit-shots are needed. And if you stalk through heavy brush, be prepared to snapshoot.

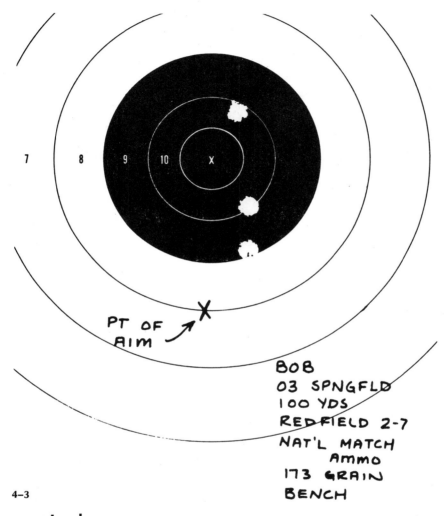

PT OF AIM

X

BOB
03 SPNGFLD
100 YDS
REDFIELD 2-7
NAT'L MATCH
AMMO
173 GRAIN
BENCH

4–3

Lead

A few words are in order about shooting at running game and about snapshooting in particular. Snapshooting is the fine art of seeing a target (usually moving), raising your rifle, and firing just after the rifle comes to rest on your shoulder all in one fluid movement. All I'll say about snapshooting is that not one hunter in fifty can do it well, and if you are not sure of yourself, forget it. Snapshooting has much in common with upland bird shooting in the type of reaction required. The main difference is that the upland shooter puts out a large shot pattern while the rifle-toting deer hunter fires a single round and hence has a much smaller margin for error.

Shots at moving game in which the hunter has a somewhat longer time to set up, say up to five seconds, are a different story. In such situations, aim can be carefully taken, the necessary lead taken, and the shot fired in a deliberate manner.

Lead is the distance that you have to aim ahead of the target to compensate for the target's movement during the bullet's flight. The amount of lead necessary for a given shot depends on three factors: the apparent speed of the target, the velocity of the bullet, and the distance to the target. The apparent speed of the target is the deer's speed perpendicular to the imaginary line drawn between the hunter and the deer. For example, if the deer is running directly toward the hunter, its apparent speed is zero and no lead is necessary. On the other hand, if the deer is running at right angles to the hunter, its apparent speed is its actual speed over the ground. If the deer is running at an angle toward or away from the hunter its apparent speed is somewhere between the two. To figure the amount of lead needed, it is necessary to know the average speed of deer in various gaits. These speeds are as follows:

Steady walk	5 feet per second
Trot	10 feet per second
Slow bounding run	25 feet per second
Fast bounding run	40 feet per second

The second factor to consider is bullet velocity. The velocity of the bullet will determine how long the bullet takes to get to the target, and this in turn will determine how much time the target has to move during the bullet's flight. Note that you cannot take the muzzle velocity of the caliber and load that you are using and use the muzzle velocity as the bullet velocity since the bullet slows down as it travels. The best way to determine bullet velocity is to look it up in tables. As an example, consider the two deer cartridges below.

	VELOCITY (FPS)			
CARTRIDGE/WEIGHT	MUZZLE	100 YDS.	200 YDS.	300 YDS.
.30/06, 180 gr.	2,700	2,330	2,010	1,740
.35 Remington, 200 gr.	2,100	1,710	1,390	1,160

The 180-grain bullet from a .30/06 has a muzzle velocity of 2,700 fps and a velocity of 2,330 fps at 100 yards. We can say that the approximate average velocity over the first 100 yards is the average of these two numbers, 2,515 fps. This means that the bullet travels the first 100 yards in $300/2,515 = .12$ seconds. A similar computation for the .35 Remington gives the 100-yard time of flight as .16 seconds. We can see already that the amount of lead is going to differ for these two since the .35 Remington takes considerably longer to get where it's going. At this point the serious ballistics student may object that the above described averaging procedure is not exact, that muzzle velocity depends on barrel length, and time of flight depends on bullet shape. All of which is very true, but the above figures and methods are good enough for the hunter's purposes.

Now for the actual computation of lead. Say you are participating in a deer drive. The drive boss has positioned you and your trusty .30/06 on a high rock ledge overlooking a grassy opening. You suddenly hear a noise to your right and about 100 yards away a big fat six-pointer trots out of the woods walking at right angles to you. You whip out your ballistics tables, two slide rules, and a desk calculator, average up the velocities, calculate the bullet's time of flight as .12 seconds, and look up to see that the deer is now half way across the opening. Next you pull out your dog-eared and worn copy of this book and find out that a trotting deer moves at 10 fps. You then multiply .12 seconds by 10 fps and find out that the lead needed is 1.2 feet or about 1 foot and 2 inches. You then raise your trusty shooting iron, and look through the scope just in time to see a white tail disappear into the woodline.

Several lessons should be learned from this experience. First of all, even at relatively short ranges such as 100 yards and with relatively slow-moving targets, a lot of lead is required in spite of the fact that the cartridge was the fairly fast stepping .30/06. Neglecting this lead could result in a paunch-shot cripple or a miss. Secondly, the amount of lead required and the estimation of deer speeds and ranges must be second nature to the hunter who plans to shoot at moving targets. If you can't do it quickly and accurately either practice some more or forget about it. You must know in advance the time of flight of your bullet to various ranges, and you must be able to estimate the deer's speed quickly. The following chapter gives flight times for most popular deer cartridges.

Finally, you must practice beforehand on moving targets. Some rifle clubs have such facilities. The deer outline pulled along on a trolley is helpful, but my favorite is the old tire target. This target consists of an old tire with a circular piece of cardboard inserted between the sidewalls to fill the center hole completely. A bull's-eye is painted on the piece of cardboard. The tire is then rolled down a hillside and the rifleman tries to hit the bullseye. On proper terrain the tire bounces as it rolls in a manner reminiscent of a bounding deer. The cost is approximately nothing.

Now that you know all about the theory behind computing lead, let's put a few restrictions on where you use it. Most hunters couldn't hit a 747 taxiing down a runway at distances of greater

4-4 A target taped to a piece of cardboard inserted between the sidewalls of an old tire makes an excellent target for practice shots on running game. Just roll the target down a rough hillside, and the bouncing motion that results is similar to that of a running deer.

than 150 yards. I don't recommend shooting at deer at ranges greater than about 150 yards if their apparent speed is faster than a walk. If you decide that your lead is more than about two feet, pass up that shot too. It is very difficult to estimate lead accurately when the point of aim is not on the animal. If an unalarmed deer is walking and you are uncertain of the lead to use, it is often helpful to sight in on him and then whistle softly or make some other slight noise. The animal will invariably freeze and look to see where the noise came from. This will give you plenty of time to fire a deliberate shot at a stationary target.

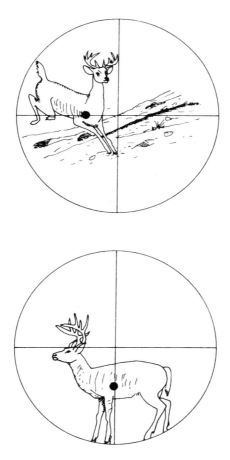

4–5 Lead (upper figure) is the distance you must aim and shoot ahead of the target to account for the movement of the target during the bullet's flight. Holdover (lower figure) is the distance you must aim and shoot over the target to account for the drop of the bullet as it travels to the target.

Holdover

Holdover is the distance that you have to aim above the point you want to hit to compensate for bullet drop. Luckily for the hunter, he is not interested in target-shooting accuracy. This simplifies his problem when it comes to bullet-drop considerations.

Figure 4–6 shows the trajectory followed by a 160-grain .270 Winchester bullet relative to the shooter's line of sight. It is assumed that the rifle has a scope mounted one-and-a-half inches above the bore and that the gun is zeroed at 200 yards. Note that the bullet starts out one-and-a-half inches low, rises up through the line of sight at about 28.5 yards, reaches a maximum of about two inches above the line of sight at 100 yards, and drops back down to the point of aim at 200 yards since this is where the gun is zeroed. The bullet then continues to drop and at 250 yards is six inches low and at 400 yards is twenty-five inches low. Recall that earlier I said that the hunter only needs to be able to keep his shots in a twelve-inch circle for standing broadside shots. If he aims at the center of this circle, he has a six-inch leeway, high and low. Since the 160-grain bullet just discussed never strays from the line of sight by more than six inches out to 250 yards, the hunter can shoot at targets up to 250 yards away without having to hold over. The maximum distance to which one can neglect holdover depends on both caliber and bullet weight. The following chapter gives recommended sighting-in distances for all common deer cartridges and gives the maximum no-holdover range for each. In addition, bullet drops at greater ranges are given. The once-a-year hunter should stick to one or two bullet weights and memorize the drop figures for those bullets. Also, it wouldn't hurt to write the figures down and tape them to your stock or scope. Then, if you were using the .270 Winchester cartridge depicted in Figure 4–6, you would know immediately that if you estimate the deer's range as 300 yards, you should aim about ten inches above the point that you want to hit. This means you should lay the horizontal crosshair (if you are using a crosshair scope) just about even with the deer's back.

Range Estimation

As mentioned previously, range estimation is a vital part of determining both lead and holdover. Unfortunately, range estimation becomes increasingly difficult as the range increases, and it is at the longer ranges where accurate estimation becomes more critical. With a little practice, most people can estimate 100 yards fairly accurately. But the next two 100-yard increments are much tougher. There are several reasons why this is so. For one thing, part of the

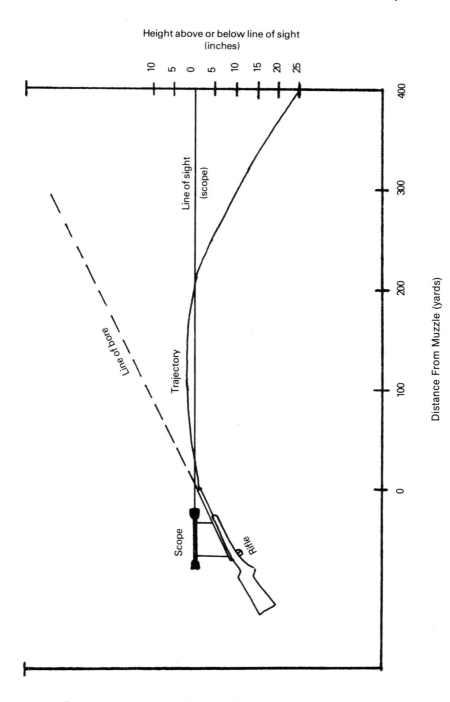

4–6   Bullet Trajectory relative to line of sight

information that the brain uses to estimate distances comes from man's stereo vision—his eyes are separated. A person with one eye has great difficulty estimating ranges. At distances of several feet, the separation distance of your eyes is fairly great compared to the distance that you are estimating. But as the object whose distance you are trying to estimate recedes further and further away, your eyes seem to converge into a single point. At 400 yards, your stereo vision provides little assistance.

Another reason why long distances are difficult to estimate is that as the distances become greater, your vision is skimming across the surface of the ground. You see the distance you are trying to estimate "on edge" so to speak. On flat ground, you might have great difficulty estimating 300 yards accurately, whereas a helicopter pilot hovering above you could do it much more easily since he is looking down on the distance to be estimated. This is why it is easier to estimate distances from a tree stand than from a standing position on the ground.

A third reason for the difficulty of estimating ranges is that your brain also uses the decrease in an object's size to compute its distance, and the decrease in size becomes relatively less important for succeeding increments of distance. If an 1,800-pound bull moose is so close that he is standing on your toe, his hulking smelly presence is painfully obvious. If he has moved out to 100 yards, the decrease in his size is quite dramatic. If, however, he has moved out another 100 yards, the decrease is less dramatic. And when he has moved from 500 to 600 yards, you'll have to watch closely to see any diffference at all.

The increasing difficulty of determining range with increasing distance is unfortunate because bullets drop drastically at the longer ranges. For example, if you are hunting with a .308 Winchester with 150-grain bullets zeroed at 250 yards and estimate the range to be 300 yards when in fact it is 400 yards, your shot will wind up 15.5 inches lower than you planned—a nice clean miss.

Like any other hunting or shooting skill, range estimation ability can be improved with practice. The best way to do this is to practice taking a measured stride until you are reasonably sure that you can take the same number of steps to cover a given distance— say fifty-three steps to fifty yards. Then go out into the woods and practice estimating distances to trees, stumps, bushes, and the like. Pace the distance off and see how close you were. A little practice would make you fairly competent at distances up to 150 or 200 yards.

Longer distances are best estimated in terms of some standard length with which you are familiar, for example, the length of a football field or the length of the block on which you live. You then lay this distance out mentally on the ground between you and the target. If the distance looks like two-and-a-half football fields, you have an estimate of the range, and the accuracy of the estimate depends on the accuracy of your concept of a football field. By now you are probably beginning to see the value of a cartridge that allows you to shoot at ranges up to 250 yards without having to estimate range and apply holdover. The vast majority of all whitetail deer are shot at ranges less than 250 yards.

There is a good way to get around range estimation in some cases. If you are the kind of hunter who likes to take a stand and wait for game to go by, it is a simple matter to pace off beforehand the distance to all critical trails and other landmarks in your area of visibility. Then when the game appears, there is no estimating to be done. You know the ranges. You can even take this one step further. I have several favorite stands around which I've paced off distances. Occasionally before I take a stand I'll tack six-inch bullseyes to trees at varying distances and in various directions around the stand. Then, when the day is over, if I haven't gotten my deer, I fire one shot on each bullseye. The shots are rarely other than solid hits. If you know the range and know your gun, there's no reason why they shouldn't be.

If you hunt in areas that require a lot of over-200-yard shots (and very, very few hunters do) you might consider getting a scope with a built-in range-finding device or an auxiliary range-finder. (Range-finder scopes, which can be helpful at long ranges, are discussed in Chapter 6).

5

Rifles and Shotguns

When the deer hunter sets out to select a rifle or shotgun, he is really embarking upon a three-part process. First, he must make a choice of cartridge. Does he prefer a .30/06 or a .30/30? Once the cartridge type is selected, a rifle action must be chosen. Does the hunter prefer lever, automatic, or bolt actions? In some cases the cartridge selection will partially or completely determine the action. For example, some of the most popular lever actions do not come chambered for cartridges with pointed bullets. The last step in the gun-selection process is the choice of suitable sights. Steps one and two, selection of the cartridge and action, are treated in this chapter. The third step, sight selection, is covered in the next chapter.

Rifle Cartridges

When I first got into the sport of deer hunting, I was young and impressionable and I spent countless hours poring over ballistics data searching for the caliber that was exactly right for me. How did the .270 Winchester with 150-grain bullets stack up against the .30/06 with the same bullet weight? What about the sectional density and midrange trajectory? How about residual energy at 400 yards? (Incidently, I've never shot at a whitetail that far away and have not even seen very many at that range.) Would I be better off with the .257 Roberts for long shots? And so the comparisons went on.

But with the passing years, I have grown a little less industrious, a little smarter, and a lot slower afoot. These tired old eyeballs don't like reading all those little numbers anymore, and I've begun to question just what they mean anyway. There was a time when I thought that 1,200 foot-pounds was a magic number for residual bullet energy. Anything less than that just wouldn't do the job consistently on deer. Then I found out somewhere that Daniel Boone dropped more deer than I'll ever see with a muzzle-loader that churned up no more than 900 foot-pounds at the muzzle. So much for that sacred cow.

I have come to believe that there are any number of calibers around that will do the job quite adequately, and that it probably doesn't make two cents' worth of difference whether you use a .300 Savage, a .30/06, or a .308 Winchester. There are, of course, certain generalizations that can be made concerning the effectiveness of different cartridges in brush, at long ranges, and in other specialized situations. But within any category, for example in the long-range category, I would not lose long hours of sleep fretting over the distinction between a .270 Winchester with 130-grain bullets and the .257 Roberts with 100-grain projectiles. The distinction is too subtle to have much impact on the average deer hunter. I would worry more about where on the deer I placed the bullet.

Before discussing the various cartridges and how they perform, let's say a word or two about how they are named. I will begin by letting the reader in on a big secret about the Clear and Precise Universal System of Cartridge Nomenclature (CPUSCN). The big secret is that there isn't one. There are hundreds of ways to name cartridges. The first number in the cartridge designation is usually related to the diameter of your rifle bore. In some cases the number is the bore diameter in hundredths or thousandths of an inch, and in some cases it's the groove diameter. The .270 Winchester has a bore diameter of .270 inches, whereas the .308 Winchester has a groove diameter of .308 inches. In other cases the designer

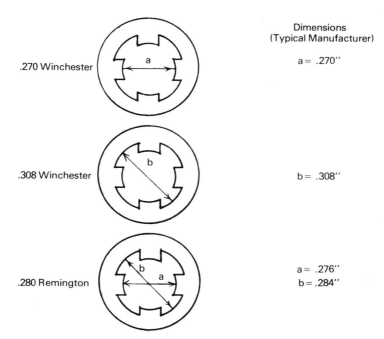

.270 Winchester

.308 Winchester

.280 Remington

Dimensions
(Typical Manufacturer)

a = .270″

b = .308″

a = .276″
b = .284″

5–1   Groove and Land Dimensions

just couldn't make up his mind; hence, we have the .280 Remington with a bore diameter of .276 inches and groove diameter of .284 inches. You will be delighted to know that the system for the rest of the cartridge designation is equally consistent. The .257 Roberts was developed by a charcoal burner named Roberts. The .300 Savage was so named to give the Savage Arms Company a little free publicity every time the designation was used. The second "30" in .30/30 means that the cartridge was commonly loaded with 30 grains of powder. The "3,000" in .250/3,000 means that the cartridge was commonly loaded to give a muzzle velocity of about 3,000 feet per second. The "06" in .30/06 refers to the year, 1906, in which this fine old cartridge was adopted by the Armed Forces. Such names as Hornet, Jet, and Varmintmaster do absolutely nothing that I can discern except possibly impress hunters. As one would expect in such a matter, the Europeans have their own system of nomenclature. Thus a 7 × 57 Mauser has a seven-millimeter bore diameter and the length of the cartridge case is fifty-seven millimeters.

In selecting a deer cartridge from the vast array of commercial cannon fodder that is available, certain cartridges can be eliminated immediately because of insufficient killing power. I would not recommend to a serious deer hunter any caliber less than .25. This recommendation will no doubt cause the six-millimeter boys to fall out of their tree stands. I am well aware that a lot of venison has been put on the meat pole with a .243 Winchester and the 6mm Remington. But these calibers have always seemed to me to be compromises for shooting at woodchuck or deer. A compromise between a woodchuck and a deer in size is about the size of a coyote, and that's just about what these two cartridges are right for—coyote. The foregoing discussion is not, of course, meant to imply that any caliber .25 inches or bigger is adequate for deer. Stay away from the .25/20 WCF, the .30 Carbine, the .32/20 WCF, and the .32/40 Winchester.

At the other end of the spectrum, one would do well to forget about the "super heavies." If you walked out into the deer woods with a .458 Winchester, you would probably get a few deer (and maybe a few hunters) that just plain died of fright. It might at first seem that too much gun shouldn't hurt, but this is not the case. High-power cartridges meant for the biggest and most dangerous game are designed to penetrate deep and expand slowly. They'll zip right through a skinny little whitetail and expend most of their energy knocking down trees and hills on the far side of the critter. For deer hunting, don't consider anything heavier than .35 caliber. The most notable exception is the .444 Marlin, which is an adequate deer cartridge. The only other possible exceptions to this rule are the obsolete .38/40 Winchester, the .38/55 Winchester, the .44/40 Winchester, and the .45/70, all of which have trajectories like basketballs. If your great granddad didn't hand one down to you and you are not a nostalgia buff, I would advise against going out and buying one for deer hunting.

Now that the field has been narrowed down to the range of .25 to .35 caliber, how can the hunter choose among all the contenders that are left? Part of the answer to that question can be ob-

5-2 This cutaway view of a .30/06 Remington "Core-Lokt" cartridge reveals construction similar to that of most modern high-power cartridges. The firing pin of the rifle strikes and ignites the primer. The ignition of the primer sends a burst of hot gases through the flash hole thereby igniting the main powder charge. The expanding hot gases produced by the burning of the main powder charge propel the bullet down the barrel. (Courtesy of Remington)

tained by considering the terrain in which you will be hunting. In some areas shots over 100 yards are seldom presented, and in such circumstances the rainbow trajectory of a cartridge such as the .35 Remington would not be objectionable. In the open ranges of the West, a flat-shooting cartridge like the .270 Winchester would be much more desirable. If the gun you plan to buy will also be used on varmints or some other game, you should insure that the cartridge you are considering comes loaded in an appropriate weight. Just remember, though, that primary consideration should be given to the gun's adequacy for deer.

A well-behaved deer bullet does not explode upon contact like a varmint round and leave a surface wound four inches in diameter and three inches deep. On the other hand, it doesn't go right through the animal and depart the far side taking most of its energy with it. The bullet should expand in a controlled fashion to .4 or .5 inches and leave most of its energy in the deer's boiler room. Some gun nuts will tell you that the bullet should come to rest just under the hide on the far side of the animal and this way it will leave all its energy in the beast and do the most damage. I would prefer to see the bullet leave a nice big exit wound on the far side, even if this means taking a few foot-pounds along with the bullet as it departs. A gun whose bullet barely penetrates the deer on a broadside shot is marginally sized for angling or quartering shots, and exit wounds make for easier tracking and more obvious blood trails should tracking be necessary.

For a number of years, hunters and sports writers have credited certain cartridges with having a greater ability to plough through brush and leaves. Generally it was felt that the heavier, slower-moving projectiles, such as the 200-grain bullet from the .35 Remington, did a better job of penetrating brush than did such projectiles as the light, fast-stepping 130-grain bullet from a .270 Winchester. Recent tests and research cast doubt on this whole supposition. There is now reason to believe that the traditional "brush busters" may not be much, if any, better than the faster, lighter bullets. In the remainder of this chapter I will point out those cartridges that conventional wisdom has long held to be superior in heavy cover. But I hasten to point out that the jury is still out on this issue.

The following table lists the better deer cartridges available today in commercial loadings with a brief categorization of each as short, medium, or long range and an indication of whether the cartridge has traditionally been considered to be a good brush-bucker. To avoid making the table unnecessarily long, only the best bullet weights for deer are shown in each cartridge. Within a cartridge type, for example the .308 Winchester, the lighter bullets of those shown to tend to shoot flatter and expand better on light game such as deer.

Effective Deer Cartridges

CARTRIDGE	BULLET WEIGHT (GRAINS)	USE
.250 Savage	100	Medium
.257 Roberts	117	Short
6.5 mm Remington Magnum	120	Long
.264 Winchester Magnum	140	Ultra-long
.270 Winchester	130	Ultra-long
	150	Long, brush
7 mm Remington Magnum	125	Ultra-long
	150	Ultra-long
	175	Long
7 mm Weatherby Magnum	139	Ultra-long
	154	Ultra-long
7x57 Mauser	139	Ultra-long
	150	Long
	175	Medium, brush
7.65 Argentine Mauser	150	Long
.280 Remington	150	Long, brush
	165	Medium, brush
.284 Winchester	125	Ultra-long
	150	Long, brush
.30/30 Winchester	150	Short
	170	Short, brush
.32 Winchester Special	170	Short, brush
.30 Remington	170	Short, brush
.32 Remington	170	Short, brush
.300 Savage	150	Medium
	180	Medium, brush
.30/40 Krag	180	Medium
.308 Winchester	150	Long
	180	Medium
.300 Weatherby Magnum	150	Ultra-long
	180	Ultra-long
.30/06 Springfield	150	Long
	180	Long, brush
.300 H&H Magnum	150	Ultra-long
	180	Ultra-long
.300 Winchester Magnum	150	Ultra-long
	180	Ultra-long
.303 British	130	Long
	150	Long
	180	Medium, brush
.303 Savage	180	Short, brush
	190	Short, brush
8 mm Mauser	170	Short
.338 Winchester Magnum	200	Ultra-long
.348 Winchester	200	Long
.340 Weatherby Magnum	200	Ultra-long
.35 Remingtom	200	Short, brush
.358 Winchester	200	Medium
.350 Remington Magnum	200	Long
.444 Marlin	240	Medium, brush

The heavier bullets have more arched trajectories and some claim that they will penetrate brush better. Care must be taken with the heavier bullets to insure selection of a tip that will expand well on the light body of a deer. For these reasons, the deer hunter who is not confronted with excessive brush will do well to choose the 150-grain loads for such cartridges as the .30/06 and the .303 British instead of the heavier bullets.

Never one to be timid, I will foolhardily wade right in to make some generalized recommendations about cartridges based on the type of hunting that you expect to encounter. For deer hunting over the 70 percent of the country where extremely long-range shots are rarely encountered, you would be well armed with any of the following:

.264 Winchester Magnum	.284 Winchester
.270 Winchester	7x57 Mauser
.280 Remington	.308 Winchester
.30/06 Springfield	.300 Winchester Magnum
.303 British	

Ultra-long-range shooting to me means pushing shots out to 300 or 400 yards. Most hunters can't even see that far, most cartridges have very arched trajectories at those ranges, and something like one deer in a thousand is brought down at such distances. But if you think it's necessary, try one of these:

.264 Winchester Magnum	.270 Winchester
.270 Weatherby	7 mm Remington Magnum
7 mm Weatherby Magnum	7x57 Mauser
.280 Remington	.284 Winchester
.300 Winchester Magnum	

And if you have some masochistic compulsion to shoot through wood piles and brush to get your deer, rather than use a traditional "brush bucker," I would recommend that you use a shotgun. (Shotguns are discussed later in this chapter.)

Within each of the above categories, other cartridges could have been included. But those shown were selected based on general flexibility of the cartridge. The hunter who selects one of these cartridges will not be stuck with an overly specialized "one hunting condition" gun. For example, the .35 Remington is a fine short-range weapon if you happen to have one lying around. But if you don't, I wouldn't recommend that you go out and buy one for deer hunting since there are plenty of other good guns around that don't have such limited range.

Trajectory and Sighting Data

CARTRIDGE	BULLET WTS. GRS.	SHORT RANGE YARDS						LONG RANGE YARDS						
		50	100	150	200	250	300	100	150	200	250	300	400	500
250 Savage Super-X	87	0.5	0.9	0	−2.3	−6.1	−11.8	2.0	1.7	0	−3.3	−8.4	−25.2	−53.4
250 Savage Super-X	100	0.2	0	−1.6	−4.9	−10.0	−17.4	2.4	2.0	0	−3.9	−10.1	−30.5	−65.2
256 Winchester Mag. Super-X	60	0.3	0	−2.3	−7.3	−15.9	−29.6	1.5	0	−4.2	−12.1	−25.0	−72.1	−157.2
257 Roberts Super-X	87	0.4	0.8	0	−2.0	−5.5	−10.6	1.8	1.5	0	−3.0	−7.5	−22.7	−48.0
257 Roberts Super-X	100	0.6	1.0	0	−2.5	−6.9	−13.2	2.3	1.9	0	−3.7	−9.4	−28.6	−60.9
257 Roberts Super-X	117	0.3	0	−1.9	−5.8	−11.9	−20.7	2.9	2.4	0	−4.7	−12.0	−36.7	−79.2
264 Winchester Mag. Super-X	100	0.2	0.5	0	−1.5	−4.1	−7.9	2.1	2.4	1.8	0	−3.0	−13.6	−31.9
264 Winchester Mag. Super-X	140	0.4	0.7	0	−1.9	−4.9	−9.4	2.7	3.0	2.1	0	−3.5	−15.0	−33.7
270 Winchester Super-X	100	0.3	0.6	0	−1.6	−4.5	−8.7	2.4	2.7	1.9	0	−3.3	−15.0	−35.2
270 Winchester Super-X	130	0.4	0.7	0	−1.9	−5.1	−9.7	1.7	1.4	0	−2.7	−6.8	−19.9	−40.5
270 Winchester Super-X	150	0.6	0.9	0	−2.3	−6.1	−11.7	2.1	1.7	0	−3.3	−8.2	−24.1	−49.4
284 Winchester Super-X	125	0.4	0.8	0	−2.0	−5.3	−10.1	1.7	1.5	0	−2.8	−7.2	−21.1	−43.7
284 Winchester Super-X	150	0.6	1.0	0	−2.4	−6.3	−12.1	2.1	1.8	0	−3.4	−8.5	−24.8	−51.0
7 MM Mauser (7 × 57) Super-X	175	0.4	0	−2.2	−6.6	−13.4	−23.0	1.5	0	−3.6	−9.7	−18.6	−46.8	−92.8
7 MM Remington Mag. Super-X	125	0.3	0.6	0	−1.7	−4.7	−9.1	2.5	2.8	2.0	0	−3.4	−15.0	−34.5
7 MM Remington Mag. Super-X	150	0.4	0.8	0	−1.9	−5.2	−9.9	1.7	1.5	0	−2.8	−7.0	−20.5	−42.1
7 MM Remington Mag. Super-X	175	0.2	0	−1.5	−4.6	−9.4	−16.3	2.3	1.9	0	−3.7	−9.4	−28.2	−59.5
30 Carbine	110	0.9	0	−4.5	−13.5	−28.3	−49.9	0	−4.5	−13.5	−28.3	−49.9	−118.6	−228.1
30-30 Winchester Super-X	150	0.5	0	−2.6	−7.7	−16.0	−27.9	1.7	0	−4.3	−11.6	−22.7	−59.1	−120.5
30-30 Winchester Super-X	170	0.6	0	−3.0	−8.9	−18.0	−31.1	2.0	0	−4.8	−13.0	−25.1	−63.6	−126.7
30 Remington Super-X	170	0.7	0	−3.3	−9.7	−19.6	−33.8	2.2	0	−5.3	−14.1	−27.2	−69.0	−136.9
30-06 Springfield Super-X	110	0.4	0.7	0	−2.0	−5.6	−11.1	1.7	1.5	0	−3.1	−8.0	−25.5	−57.4
30-06 Springfield Super-X	125	0.4	0.8	0	−2.1	−5.6	−10.7	1.8	1.5	0	−3.0	−7.7	−23.0	−48.5
30-06 Springfield Super-X	150	0.6	1.0	0	−2.4	−6.6	−12.7	2.2	1.8	0	−3.5	−9.0	−27.0	−57.1
30-06 Springfield Super-X	180	0.2	0	−1.8	−5.5	−11.2	−19.5	2.7	2.3	0	−4.4	−11.3	−34.4	−73.7
30-06 Springfield Super-X	220	0.4	0	−2.3	−6.8	−13.8	−23.6	1.5	0	−3.7	−9.9	−19.0	−47.4	−93.1
30-40 Krag Super-X	180	0.4	0	−2.4	−7.1	−14.5	−25.0	1.6	0	−3.9	−10.5	−20.3	−51.7	−103.9

Cartridge	Bullet (grs.)													
30-40 Krag Super-X	220	0.6	0	-2.9	-8.2	-16.4	-27.6	1.9	0	-4.4	-11.6	-21.9	-53.3	-101.8
300 Winchester Mag. Super-X	150	0.3	0.7	0	-1.8	-4.8	-9.3	2.6	2.9	2.1	0	-3.5	-15.4	-35.5
300 Winchester Mag. Super-X	180	0.5	0.8	0	-2.0	-5.3	-10.1	1.8	1.5	0	-2.8	-7.0	-20.2	-40.7
300 Winchester Mag. Super-X	220	0.2		-1.7	-4.9	-9.9	-16.9	2.5	2.0	0	-3.8	-9.5	-27.5	56.1
300 H&H Magnum Super-X	150	0.4	0.8	0	-2.0	-5.3	-10.1	1.7	1.5	0	-2.8	-7.2	-21.2	-43.8
300 H&H Magnum Super-X	180	0.6	0.9	0	-2.3	-6.0	-11.5	2.1	1.7	0	-3.2	-8.0	-23.3	-47.4
300 H&H Magnum Super-X	220	0.3	0	-1.9	-5.5	-11.0	-18.7	2.7	2.2	0	-4.2	-10.5	-30.7	-63.0
300 Savage Super-X	150	0.3	0	-1.9	-5.7	-11.6	-19.9	2.8	2.3	0	-4.5	-11.5	-34.4	-73.0
300 Savage Super-X	150	0.3	0	-1.8	-5.4	-11.0	-18.8	2.7	2.2	0	-4.2	-10.7	-31.5	-65.5
300 Savage Super-X	180	0.5	0	-2.6	-7.7	-15.6	-27.1	1.7	0	-4.2	-11.3	-21.9	-55.8	-112.0
300 Savage Super-X	180	0.4	0	-2.3	-6.7	-13.5	-22.8	1.5	0	-3.6	-9.6	-18.2	-44.1	-84.2
303 British Super-X	180	0.3	0	-2.0	-5.8	-11.6	-19.6	2.9	0	0	-4.4	-11.0	-32.0	-65.5
308 Winchester Super-X	110	0.4	0.8	0	-2.2	-6.0	-11.9	1.9	1.6	0	-3.3	-8.6	-27.4	-61.8
308 Winchester Super-X	125	0.5	0.8	0	-2.1	-5.7	-11.1	1.9	1.6	0	-3.1	-7.9	-23.7	-50.0
308 Winchester Super-X	150	0.2	0	-1.6	-4.8	-9.8	-16.9	2.4	2.0	0	-3.8	-9.8	-29.3	-62.0
308 Winchester Super-X	180	0.3	0	-2.0	-5.9	-12.1	-20.9	2.9	2.4	0	-4.7	-12.1	-36.9	-79.1
308 Winchester Super-X	200	0.4	0	-2.1	-6.3	-12.6	-21.4	1.4	0	-3.4	-9.0	-17.2	-42.1	-81.1
32 Win. Special Super-X	170	0.6	0	-3.1	-9.2	-19.0	-33.2	2.0	0	-5.1	-13.8	-27.1	-70.9	-144.3
32 Remington Super-X	170	0.7	0	-3.4	-10.2	-20.9	-36.5	2.3	0	-5.6	-15.2	-29.6	-76.7	-4.5
32-20 Winchester	100	0	-5.6	-18.8	-40.8	-72.7	-115.4	0	-10.5	-20.7	-58.8	-98.7	-215.2	-388.1
8 MM Mauser (8 × 57) Super-X	170	0.4	0	-2.3	-7.0	-14.6	-25.7	-1.6	0	-3.9	-10.7	-21.0	-55.4	-114.3
338 Winchester Mag. Super-X	200	0.5	0.9	0	-2.3	-6.1	-11.6	2.0	1.7	0	-3.2	-8.2	-24.3	-50.4
338 Winchester Mag. Super-X	250	0.2	0	-1.7	-5.2	-10.5	-18.0	2.6	2.1	0	-4.0	-10.2	-30.0	-61.9
338 Winchester Mag. Super-X	300	0.4	0	-2.3	-6.7	-13.5	-23.1	1.5	0	-3.6	-9.7	-18.6	-46.2	-90.7
348 Winchester Super-X	200	0.3	0	-2.1	-6.2	-12.7	-21.9	1.4	0	-3.4	-9.2	-17.7	-44.4	-87.9
35 Remington Super-X	200	0.8	0	-3.8	-11.3	-23.5	-41.2	2.5	0	-6.3	-17.1	-33.6	-87.7	-176.3
351 Winchester S.L.	180	0	-2.1	-7.8	-17.8	-32.9	-53.9	0	-4.7	-13.6	-27.6	-47.5	-108.8	-203.9
358 Winchester Super-X	200	0.4	0	-2.2	-6.5	-13.3	-23.0	1.5	0	-3.6	-9.7	-18.6	-47.2	-94.1

TRAJECTORY inches above (+) or below (−) line of sight. 0 = indicates yardage at which rifle is sighted in. Courtesy Winchester-Western

Approximate Time of Flight Data

CARTRIDGE	BULLET WT. (GRAINS)	MUZZLE VEL. (FPS)	TIME OF FLIGHT (SEC)		
			100 YDS	200 YDS	300 YDS
.250 Savage	100	2820	.11	.24	.39
.257 Roberts	117	2650	.12	.26	.43
6.5 MM Rem. Mag.	120	3030	.10	.22	.35
.264 Winchester	140	3200	.10	.20	.32
.270 Winchester	130	3140	.10	.21	.33
	150	2900	.11	.24	.38
7 MM Rem. Mag.	125	3430	.09	.20	.31
	175	2860	.11	.23	.36
7 MM Weatherby	139	3300	.10	.20	.32
	154	3160	.10	.21	.33
7x57 Mauser	139	2660	.12	.25	.40
	150	2756	.11	.24	.37
	175	2470	.13	.28	.45
7.65 MM Mauser	150	2920	.11	.23	.36
.280 Remington	150	2900	.11	.23	.35
	165	2820	.11	.24	.38
.284 Winchester	125	3200	.10	.21	.33
	150	2900	.11	.23	.36
.30/30 Win.	150	2390	.14	.30	.49
	170	2220	.15	.32	.51
.32 Win. Spcl.	170	2250	.14	.31	.51
.30 Remington	170	2120	.15	.33	.54
.32 Remington	170	2120	.15	.33	.54
.300 Savage	150	2630	.12	.26	.41
	180	2350	.13	.28	.45
.30/40 Krag	180	2470	.13	.28	.46
.308 Winchester	150	2820	.11	.24	.34
	180	2620	.12	.27	.43
.300 Weatherby	150	3545	.09	.19	.30
	180	3245	.10	.20	.32
.30/06 Sprfld.	150	2910	.11	.23	.37
	180	2700	.12	.24	.38
.300 H&H	150	3190	.10	.21	.33
	180	2920	.11	.22	.35
.300 Win. Mag.	150	3400	.09	.20	.31
	180	3070	.10	.21	.33
.303 British	150	2720	.12	.25	.39
	180	2540	.12	.26	.41
.303 Savage	180	2140	.15	.33	.54
	190	1980	.16	.36	.58
8 MM Mauser	170	2510	.13	.29	.48
.338 Win. Mag.	200	3000	.11	.22	.35
.348 Winchester	200	2530	.13	.27	.43
.340 Weatherby	200	3210	.10	.21	.33
.35 Remington	200	2080	.16	.35	.59
.358 Winchester	200	2530	.13	.27	.44
.350 Rem. Mag.	200	2710	.12	.25	.40

The Trajectory and Sighting Table gives recommended sighting-in distances for most popular deer cartridges and provides useful trajectory information for the deer hunter. The recommended sighting-in distances are chosen specifically to minimize the need for holdover. The table just above gives time-of-flight data to aid in the calculation of lead. (See Chapter 4 for a discussion of holdover and lead.)

Rifle Actions

The deer hunter has his choice of four basic types of rifle actions:

5–3 Bolt-actions are the most accurate and reliable of all rifle actions. Bolt-action rifles are available for most cartridges of interest to the deer hunter. Manufacturers of these guns offer the hunter a large selection of weights, finishes, and sights; and many come in both right-handed and left-handed models. From the top, the guns shown here are: Harrington & Richardson's Model 300, Ithaca's Model LSA-55, Mossberg's Model 810, Remington's Model 700 BDL, Savage's Model 110-C, and the Model 70 Winchester. (Courtesy of the respective manufacturers)

the bolt action, the lever action, the pump, and the semiautomatic.

The bolt action owes much of its popularity to its adoption by the military as the standard shoulder weapon of the GI. Soldiers returning from World War I and World War II were familiar with and had come to like their bolt action Krags and Springfields. When these quality Mauser-style actions were made available to the shooting public in large numbers as military surplus, the bolt action became an American shooting mainstay.

Where the utmost accuracy is needed, the bolt action rifle is unbeatable. Its accurate locking system results in precise cartridge seating shot after shot. The strength of its rotating-lug locking sys-

5–4   The lever-action rifle rates as the all-time favorite among deer hunters. It is estimated that more deer have been killed with the Model 94 Winchester, shown at the bottom of this photo, than with any other gun. From the top, the guns shown here are: Browning's BLR, Marlin's Model 336 C, Mossberg's Model 472 SCA, the Savage Model 99-C, and the Model 94 Winchester. (Courtesy of the respective manufacturers)

tem made it capable of employing cartridges that for many years could not be used in the weaker lever actions. Where utmost speed is needed (which usually it isn't), the bolt action is not as fast on repeat shots as any of the other three action types. It is, however, the strongest, most accurate, and most foolproof of all actions.

The lever action owes its popularity to two factors: its speed on repeat shots and the Model 94 Winchester. The Model 94, brought out in 1894, was the first lever action to be chambered for the new smokeless cartridges. The light weight of this rifle and the popularity of the .30/30 cartridge for which it is chambered have made the Model 94 the most popular deer rifle of all time.

Shortcomings of such lever actions as the Model 94 are its two-piece stock, its tubular magazine, and its locking mechanism. The two-piece stock may work loose and becoming shaky on older rifles. The tubular magazine precludes the use of sharp-nosed bullets, such as the .270 Winchester, since the primer of one cartridge would rest on the pointed nose of the next cartridge and there would be danger of accidental firing if the gun were dropped or jolted. The locking mechanism precludes the use of the new high-intensity cartridges. In newer lever actions, such as the Model 88 Winchester, all of these objections have been overcome. The stock is one piece, the bolt is a new rotating design, and the magazine is clip fed. Although this model has been discontinued by the manufacturer, it is available in used condition. Chambered for a versatile cartridge such as the .308 Winchester, the Model 88 is a top-drawer choice for the deer hunter. Other lever actions, such as the Savage Model 99C, although having two-piece stocks, come chambered for high-powered cartridges and are also good choices for the deer hunter who fancies this type of action.

The slide-action rifle gained much of its initial popularity with shotgunners who were familiar with and liked the slide-action smoothbore. Initially the gun had many of the same disadvantages as the lever action, but like the lever action the slide action now has a rotating bolt-locking system and a clip-fed action.

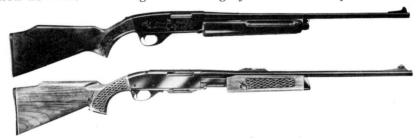

5–5 Slide-action rifles are favored by some rifle hunters who have become comfortable with slide actions in shotguns. Shown here from the top are the Savage Model 170 and the Remington Model 760 BDL Deluxe. (Courtesy of Savage and Remington)

The one disadvantage that remains is the two-piece stock. On some models the slide becomes loose, making a steady hold difficult.

John M. Browning was a gun-designing genius. The auto-loading rifle action that he designed just after the turn of the century is still with us today in slightly modified form. For quick follow-up shots, nothing beats a semiautomatic. Semiautomatic actions are somewhat prone to malfunctions, but unless you plan to drive tent stakes or dig for clams with your rifle these actions will do quite nicely.

5–6 Automatic rifles have not traditionally been very popular with American hunters. This reaction stems in part from the greater complexity of these guns, which gives them a somewhat higher probability of malfunction than guns with simpler actions such as the bolt action. However, if quick follow-up shots are of paramount importance to the hunter, these guns merit serious consideration. From the top, the guns shown here are: the Browning Automatic Rifle, the Model 360 Harrington & Richardson, and the Model 742 BDL Remington. (Courtesy of the respective manufacturers)

After all this pleasant small talk about actions, I propose to stick my neck out again with some fearless specific suggestions on actions.

As you no doubt gathered from the last chapter, I place very little store in follow-up shots. I like the first one to do the job. Therefore it should come as no surprise that I don't care if the bolt action is a little slower. In view of its other advantages, I like it. Call it unreasoning emotionalism if you like. In fact, I have even flirted with single-shot smokepoles like the Ruger Number One. There are no doubt alarmists in the crowd who will claim that this is foolhardy and possibly inhumane if more than one shot is needed to dispatch your game. But I'm not so sure. I've often wondered if there wouldn't be fewer cripples running around in the deer woods if every hunter knew from the start that he was going to get only one shot and that he had to make it count. The last four deer I've shot were all dropped with a single round. And the one out of the last five deer that I used three rounds on, I'm convinced didn't need all that firepower. I think I put the last two shots into a deer that was dead on his feet and was too dumb to know it. Examination of the carcass revealed that any one of the three shots probably would have been lethal.

If you really think you need fast follow-ups and you are good at this type of shooting, try a semiautomatic in one of the versatile cartridges so you won't be stuck with a Johnny-One-Note rifle. The .270 Winchester, .30/06, and the .308 Winchester are all available in semiautomatics. Try one.

Shotgun Cartridges

If you are itching to try out your favorite smoothbore on deer, or if you are required by law in your area to use shotguns on deer, you'll find the choice of cartridges much simpler for shotguns than for rifles. There simply aren't so many shotgun loadings around.

Shotgun cartridges, or shells as they are commonly called, are named according to a different system from that used for rifle cartridges. Commonly available in this country are the 10, 12, 16, 20, 28, and .410 gauge shotguns. If one were to take twelve lead balls the diameter of a 12-gauge shotgun bore and weigh them, one would find that they weigh approximately one pound. Similarly sixteen balls of 16 gauge, twenty of 20 gauge, and twenty-eight of 28 gauge would weigh one pound. Thus as the gauge number goes up, bore diameter goes down. The .410 is not really a gauge but is the caliber or bore diameter in inches. The bore diameters of the various gauges in inches are:

GAUGE	BORE DIAMETER
10	.775″
12	.729″
16	.652″
20	.615″
28	.550″
.410	.410″

Shells in each gauge come in two different loadings, standard and magnum. Guns chambered for the longer, higher-pressure magnums will safely accept standard shells, but the reverse is not true. The length of the standard and magnum shells in each gauge is:

GAUGE	STANDARD	MAGNUM
10	2 ⅞	3 ½
12	2 ¾	3
16	2 ¾	2 ¾
20	2 ¾	3
28	2 ¾	2 ¾
.410	2 ½	3

In the case of the 16 and 28 gauges, the magnum loadings are packed into the standard-length shell. In addition, some manufacturers load magnum shells for the other gauges in short shells. If your gun is chambered for the long shells, it's safe to use either. If it is chambered for short shells and you have any doubts, check with a gunsmith before feeding it the short magnums. By the way, the length of the shell is its length after it has been fired and the crimped part of the shell unravels in the chamber. A 2¾-inch, 12-gauge shell measures about 2⅜ inches long before firing.

As with rifle cartridges, the hunter is given a choice in the type of projectile he wants. The only projectiles of interest to the deer hunter are 0 buckshot, 00 buckshot, and rifled slugs. I for one am not very enthusiastic about the use of buckshot on deer. I strongly suspect that there are a lot of deer brought to considerable grief every year by virtue of being perforated with a few nonlethal pieces of buckshot. In some areas, local laws allow only buckshot for deer hunting. Here the hunter has no choice. In other areas the vegetation is so dense that the hunter never takes shots over fifty yards and usually the ranges are less than that. In heavy cover such as this the hunter often gets only a brief glimpse of his game. Many areas in the South are like this. In such terrain the 12-gauge shotgun loaded with buckshot is the hunter's most lethal and consistently productive weapon. But these are very special hunting conditions and the hunter must tell himself in advance that he will have to pass up all longer shots. I would also be loathe to go out for deer with other than a 12 gauge if I were using buckshot. (The 10 gauge does not come factory loaded with buckshot. If you want to handload, be my guest—it should be potent). The factory loads with 0 and 00 buckshot in 12 gauge are:

SHELL LENGTH	SHOT SIZE	NUMBER OF PELLETS	DRAMS OF POWDER
3	00	15	4 ½
2 ¾ (Mag)	00	12	4
¾	00	9	3 ¾
2 ¾	0	12	3 ¾

The 00 buckshot pellets are .33 inches in diameter and the 0 buckshot pellets are .32 inches in diameter. The choice between 0 and 00 buckshot can be made based on the druthers of your shotgun. Some guns pattern one size better than the other. Try both in your gun. If it has a variable choke, try different choke settings. Don't worry about "shooting out the choke" with either buckshot or slugs. You won't hurt the choke. Set up a twelve-inch disk of cardboard and try blasting away at it from various ranges with different loads. See how well your gun patterns. At fifty yards, you will need a minimum of four or five pellets in the deer's vital area to be reasonably assured of a clean kill. Can you and your gun consistently deliver such patterns at the range you plan to hunt?

A shotshell loaded with a rifled slug is similar to a rifle cartridge. The projectile consists of a single piece of lead instead of some nine to fifteen pellets as in the buckshot loadings. The rifled slug stands in sharp contrast to buckshot loads when it comes to killing power. The bowling-ball-size calibers of the large slugs give them a knockdown power that is incredible. The 12-gauge slug lumbers out of the business end of a smoothbore with more than a foot-ton of energy. At fifty yards there are still 1,350 foot-pounds of energy left in this massive 415-grain, .729-caliber missile. When it connects, the rifled slug has tremendous impact. And the massive projectiles seem to do a fair job of ploughing through leaves and branches.

The main drawback of the rifled slug is its poor ballistics. Slugs have arching trajectories, lose energy rapidly, and when fired from many guns don't group well at 100 yards. At what ranges are they effective killers? I would use the 12 and 16 gauges out to a maximum of 100 yards, the 20 gauge to a maximum of 50 yards, and leave the 28 and .410 gauges at home.

Shotgun Actions

The would-be shotgun deer hunter has four common shotgun actions from which to choose. They are the break-open (single or double barrel), the automatic, the pump, and the bolt actions.

The break-open actions are available in single-barrel over/under, and the traditional side-by-side double barrel. These actions are inherently the safest of all rifle or shotgun actions. When the action is broken, there is no question about safeties being on or off or of the gun being loaded or unloaded. The chamber is visible and the gun simply can't fire. The single shot is an effective slug thrower but is not so highly recommended for buckshot, where the possibility of needing a quick second shot is somewhat higher. Both the over/under and the side-by-side are potent buckshot guns, but some guns pattern better than others. Both have a quick, almost immediate, second-shot capability. Both offer the potential for putting

5–7 Double-barrel shotguns are fine for buckshot but are not recommended for slugs since the bores of the two barrels are not exactly parallel. Shown here are the Savage Model 330 over-and-under (top) and the Savage-Fox Model B-SE side-by-side (bottom). (Courtesy of Savage)

buckshot in one barrel and a slug in the other if you are big on this sort of marksmanship hocus-pocus. I have generally found that one type of cartridge is about all that I can mentally keep track of, but I can picture situations in which the long-range slug capability would be handy in a brushy close-cover hunt. The over/under handles slugs fairly well, and with a little practice the hunter should be able to group on a billboard at 100 yards. But the side-by-side develops indigestion when fed a diet of slugs. The barrels of a side-by-side are aligned to compensate for the twisting recoil of the off-center barrels and to make the patterns from the right and left barrels cross at about forty yards. This alignment of the barrels causes the right barrel to throw a slug too far to the left and the left barrel to throw too far to the right. Some writers conclude that this means that the side-by-side is no good for slugs. I'm not so sure. I once took my 20-gauge magnum side-by-side (a honey of a shotgun!) out into the woods with a box of slugs just to see what it would do. Around the ruins of an abandoned farm I found a pail that presented a roughly ten-inch-by-ten-inch target and set it on a fence post. I paced off twenty-five yards and called in the artillery fire. After three or four shots I got so that I could hit the pail pretty regularly with the right barrel. I then switched to the left barrel and after three or four shots achieved the same degree of proficiency with it. The rest of my box of slugs was expended switching back and forth between barrels. This was a little more of a chore than shooting just one barrel, but by the time I got to the bottom of the box I was hitting on better than half of my shots. And this was with no sights other than the front bead commonly found on doubles. Had I installed a folding rear blade, possibly with two notches (one for each barrel), I am convinced that that gun would group in a twelve-inch circle at fifty yards—and possibly beyond. The effectiveness of the gun could be further improved if the hunter always fired the same barrel first.

All this discussion of cartridges invariably gets back to the question of at what range you can group your shots in a 12-inch circle with a firearm that provides adequate killing power. If you can throw folding chairs in a twelve-inch circle at 100 yards with 1,000 foot-pounds of energy, who knows . . . ?

Far and away the most popular shotguns for deer are the

5–8 If you have a 12-gauge shotgun lying around the house that you use for birds, bunnies, or other game, in all probability it will serve quite adequately as a buckshot gun. In addition, if it is not a double-barrel gun, it can probably be tailored to shoot slugs with some degree of success. All it needs is a receiver sight, a little filing on the front bead, and a lot of practice. Typical of such guns are those shown above. From the top they are: the Harrington & Richardson Model 58, the Ithaca Model 51, the Marlin 120 Magnum, the Mossberg Model 395K, the Winchester Model 1200, and the Winchester Model 37A. (Courtesy of the respective manufacturers)

semiautomatics and the pumps. The comments earlier in this chapter concerning the relative advantages of semiautomatic and pump rifles also apply to the shotguns. These guns will not only handle buckshot well, but also are made in special models designed to handle slugs. Typical of these slug guns are the Remington Model 1100 Deer Gun, the Browning Auto-5 Buck Special, the Remington Model 870 Brushmaster Deluxe, and the Ithaca Model 37 Deerslayer. The first two are semiautomatics, and the last two are pump or slide actions. Guns such as these usually come equipped with rifle-type open metallic sights, and most are adjustable for windage and elevation. Some even come equipped with a sling and quick-detachable sling swivels. These slug throwers are quite capable of grouping in a seven-inch or eight-inch circle at 100 yards in the hands of an average gunner shooting from a rest. This suffices for deer hunting, since 100 yards is about the outer range limit for slugs.

Bolt-action shotguns are smoothbores masquerading as rifles. They are safe, reliable, inexpensive, and effective but have always struck me as being oddities — like a doe with antlers. There is really no good reason why a hunter shouldn't choose such a gun for slug shooting. They are a little slow on follow-up shots. Some, like the Mossberg 395K, come equipped with rear sights.

Once again its time to hazard an opinion about gun selection to help guide the novice and bring down the scorn and ire of the experienced gun buff who hunts with a 12-gauge/16-gauge/7x57 drilling and swears that no other gun is worth taking into the woods.

If I were feeling flush with coin of the realm and were heading out to buy myself a smoothbore for use on deer, I would select a 12-gauge semiautomatic of the type specifically designed for deer. (In which case I would not really be getting a smoothbore, since these shotguns designed specifically for shooting slugs have rifled barrels. This is one of the reasons why they are more accurate with slugs than the ordinary shotgun.) I would probably wind up changing the sights and would install either a rear peep-sight well back on the receiver or a one or one-and-a-half power scope. I would zero it at 100 yards and would pour so much lead through it that my shoulder would be sore for a month. And when I headed out into the woods with it I would know that any buck that showed himself within 100 yards was searching for his eternal reward.

6

Sights for Rifles and Shotguns

Sights for deer rifles and shotguns come in two types: iron and glass. The iron sights can be further classified based on the type of rear sight used as open sights or peep sights. Most high-power rifle manufacturers decorate their products with some type of useless open rear sight. Apparently they feel some compulsion to do so on the grounds that the gun would look naked without it. But these sights are usually so much scrap iron that has to be removed and replaced by something meant for serious business, like stacking up venison. The factory-furnished sights on most guns are adequate only for very short-range cartridges.

Iron Sights

What exactly are these factory-furnished rear sights? They are usually some type of V-notch, U-notch, or buckhorn sight totally lacking windage adjustments and often adjustable only for elevation by means of a crude stepped ramp. The forward end of the sight is fitted into a dovetail, and if the weapon groups to the right or left, the appropriate correction is made by forcing the sight to the right or left with the aid of a fine-tuning instrument such as a two-pound-ball-peen hammer or a big rock. If this strikes you as less than precise, wait till you hear about the elevation adjustments. I have one little rifle the rear sight adjustment of which has a total of five steps on it. Each step moves the shot group about five inches at 100 yards. And if one of those five positions isn't right, it's too bad. If the shot group is two inches low, the next choice is three inches high!

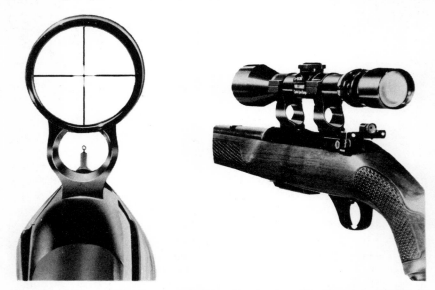

6–1 The Williams Sight-Thru mount allows the shooter either to use iron sights — by sighting below the scope — or the scope by raising his head slightly and sighting through the glass. (Courtesy of Williams)

The sight through which you view on these open rear sights is no more sophisticated than the windage and elevation adjustments. The V and U notches are difficult to get consistent sight pictures through and most hunters are unable to get deer-hunting accuracy with such sighting hardware from the prone position at ranges beyond 150 yards. The buckhorn-type rear sights have always given me sighting problems similar to those of the U and V notch, and the buckhorns have the added disadvantage of obscuring much of the target. When open rear sights are used, my favorite has always been the square notch with a front blade (flat sides and flat top on the blade). If the square notch in the rear sight is large enough to allow just a little daylight to be seen around the front blade, and if the rifle is zeroed when the top of the blade is even with the top of the square notch, I usually have a fifty-fifty chance of being able to group in a bushel basket at 100 yards.

6–2 One of the finest rear sights for the deer hunter is the adjustable aperture sight. Here the Williams Foolproof Receiver Sight is shown both detached and mounted on a rifle. Note that the sight mounted on the rifle has no disc in it. The large opening aperture is intended to give a wide field of view where pinpoint accuracy is not required. (Courtesy of Williams)

In my experience, the best iron sights are the peep sights. These sights provide a circular aperture within which the shooter centers his front sight, and peep sights are usually completely adjustable with click-type adjustments for both windage and elevation. Many of these sights come with screw-out disk apertures that are replaceable with disks of various sizes. Novices with peep sights are inclined to look through the sight, get the feeling that they are seeing all-outdoors through the disk, and run down to the local sporting goods emporium for a smaller aperture in the interests of better accuracy. In doing so, they are simply negating one of the advantages of the peep. It does give the shooter a good view of what's going on, and in spite of the wide field of view, your eye will have no trouble centering the front sight in the aperture. I have gone so far as to remove the disk altogether and just use the large residual hole. I find the added daylight a welcome relief and have no trouble getting the sight picture that I want. With a good peep sight, many hunters can keep their groups in a twelve-inch circle at 200 yards from the prone position.

Front sights are of either the blade or bead variety. I personally find the flat sides and flat top of the blade easier for my eye to define. But many prefer the bead, and it's strictly a matter of choice. Gold is a good all-round color that picks up light well and can be darkened easily with shoe polish or the smoky flame of a cigarette lighter if it must be used against a very light background such as snow. Another good color choice is red. Remember that the front sight is the weak link in your iron-sight chain and should be treated carefully. A removable hood is helpful to protect the front sight during transportation in vehicles and on rough hikes. Some hunters even leave the hood on when shooting.

Advantages of Telescopic Sights

Telescopic sights provide the hunter a tremendous advantage over his iron-sight competitors. Without such a device, the effective deer hunting range of the .32 Winchester and the 7 mm Remington Magnum are both about the same: roughly 200 yards. This is because 200 yards is about as far as the average hunter can shoot with deer-hunting accuracy with iron sights. But with telescopic sights, there is no comparison. The effective range of the .32 Winchester stays about 200 yards because of energy and trajectory limitations, but the flat-shooting Remington Magnum shoots so far that folks tell me the shooter has to take the curvature of the earth into account.

There are many advantages to using a telescopic sight, not the least of which is the magnification. If you are sighting game 400 yards away with a 4x (four power) scope, you see the game as if it were 100 yards away. This makes it much easier to get a good sight picture. The front blade or ball of iron sights would cover up the deer at 200 yards making accurate shot placement difficult. This problem is eliminated with the scope. For the early morning and late evening hunter, the scope is a great light-gathering device. Targets that would be difficult to discern in the evening light are clearly visible with a superimposed crosshair in a quality low-power scope. I have found that such a scope increases my evening hunting time by as much as half an hour. The scope also eliminates for older eyes the sighting difficulty that arises from having to focus on the front sight and the target while at least retaining an awareness of the location of the rear sight. As one's eyes become older and less flexible, such focusing becomes a bit of ocular gymnastics. When forced by a long hike or heavy load to leave your binoculars at home, the scope can also do double duty as a makeshift set of binoculars.

Telescopic sights come in a bewildering array of sizes, powers, qualities, and reticles. Many of them can be eliminated at once from the deer hunter's list of possible choices. The lightweight numbers meant for use on .22s won't stand up to the recoil of middleweight cartridges. And the high-powered, air-cooled, independently suspended scopes with electric windshield wipers have such limited fields of view that at 100 yards you would be lucky to focus on a deer's whole ankle.

Power and Eye Relief

The range of powers in which a deer hunter might possibly be interested under special circumstances is 1x to 8x. Hunters tend to overestimate the power that they need. For most hunting in the

Northeast and Southeast, a 2.5x scope is perfect. For those areas in the West and Northwest where the hunter seriously expects to encounter shots from 250 to 400 yards frequently, a 4x is preferable. Going to a higher power than necessary just cuts down on the field of view or the amount that the hunter can see through the scope at a given distance. The higher powers also magnify shake or tremble in the shooter's hold, and they don't do such a good job of light gathering. Typical rifle scopes have the fields of view indicated below at 100 yards.

POWER	FIELD (FEET)
1.5	56
2.5	43
4	30
6	20
8	15

The distance from the rearmost lens in the scope (known as the ocular lens or the ocular element) to the shooter's eye is termed eye relief. If the eye is too close or too far away from the lens, only part of the field of view is seen or else the view blacks out altogether. For a hunting scope, it is necessary that the usable eye relief cover as wide a range as possible—say, from two to five inches. If this range is too small, for example from three to four inches, the hunter's eye will have to be between three and four inches from the rear lens when he brings his rifle up, and if it is not within this

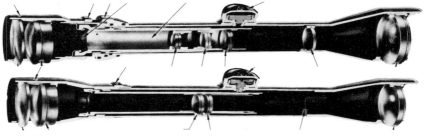

6–3 Typical lens systems for variable- and fixed-power scopes. The scopes shown are from the Williams Guide line. (Courtesy of Williams)

range, he will not be able to use the scope until he adjusts the position of his head. With the more forgiving two-to-five-inch range, he obviously has a lot more leeway, and this leeway could be critical on a fast shot. Low-power scopes have a greater eye-relief range than high-power ones, other things being equal.

If the terrain to be hunted is really variable, a variable-power scope might be just what you need. I have an old, beat-up

Springfield that I take into the woods every fall. I have a 2x ± 7x variable Redfield scope mounted on it, and that old tube has served me well over the years. I pussyfoot into the woods with it on 2x in case I need it for a fast shot, and then jack it up to 4x or more when I get to my stand. I once used it on 7x to shoot a deer standing at approximately 175 yards and did not find the high power objectionable in any way.

Reticles

The most popular reticles for big-game hunting are the crosshair, the post, and the dot. The crosshair is the favorite out West and is the one I have always found easiest to use. It is easy to pick up, facilitates leading a moving target because of its horizontal line, and masks little of the target. On the older varible scopes, the reticle used to get larger as the magnification of the scope was increased. On the newer scopes, the reticle stays the same size; and a crosshair in a variable scope is a very handy combination.

The traditional objection to the post reticle is that it masks from view much of the target if the range makes it necessary to hold over the target. This is quite important to a varmint hunter who may want to hold over a chuck at 350 yards and finds when he does so that the chuck is sitting squarely and completely behind the post. For hunters of larger game, this is not such a problem; but it is still annoying and if you want your .460 Nitro to double as a varmint gun, you would do well to steer away from the post. Someone always wants to know if this masking problem on holdover could be eliminated by rotating the scope in its mounts so that the post appears to be coming down from the top instead of up from the bottom. This would eliminate the masking problem on holdover since with the post coming down from the top you would simply hold it further above the targer to hold over. As weird as this idea is, it would probably work. The mounts for your scope might have to be shimmed since the post usually comes more than half way up into the field of view and there may not be enough adjustment in the scope to get the aiming point and the shot pattern to coincide. The elevation adjustment would now be on the bottom of the scope and might be a little hard to get at, but this is no insurmountable problem.

Dot reticles are just what the name implies: a dot suspended in an otherwise clear field. In some cases the dot is etched on glass; and in at least one case, the well-known Lee Dot Reticle, the dot is a drop of shellac suspended on tough, nearly invisible strands from the web of the black widow spider. The dot is a fairly handy reticle; it is easy to use, and it masks little of the target.

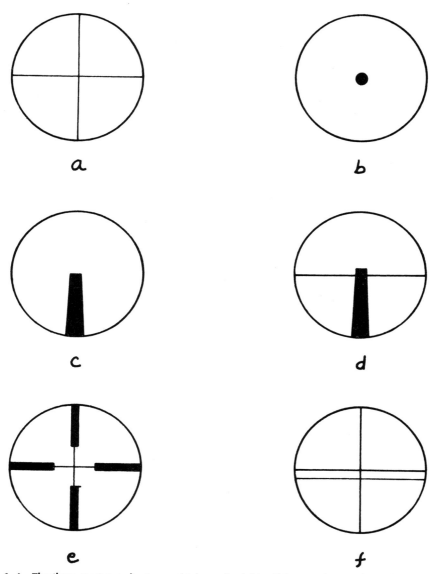

6–4   The three most popular types of telescopic sight reticles are the crosshair, the dot, and the post, shown in this figure at a, b, and c respectively. There are many variations of these three basic schemes. For example, d and e depict post-crosshair combinations. The reticle shown at f is typical of several designs that use more than one horizontal crosshair to aid in range estimation.

Range Estimation

All three of the previously discussed reticles can be used for range estimation. Range estimation with a reticle is based on the fact that a given reticle subtends a fixed angle and this translates into a fixed length per hundred yards. For example, if a dot is a two-minute

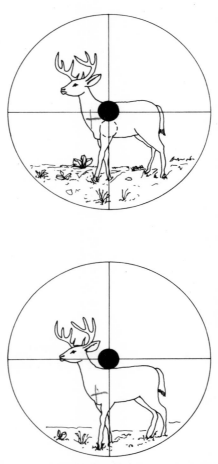

6–5   The upper figure illustrates the use of a dot reticle to estimate range. Note that the distance from the deer's back to his brisket appears to be two dots high. Since this distance is known to be about eighteen inches, that means that the dot is covering about nine inches. Assume that the dot in this reticle is a three-minute dot. Since a three-minute dot will cover three inches at one hundred yards, it will cover nine inches at three hundred yards, and therefore, the range to the deer is known to be three hundred yards. If the shooter is using .270 Winchester 160-grain cartridges, and his gun is zeroed at two hundred yards, the sight picture shown in the lower figure should be just about right to place the shot in the deer's vital area.

dot, this means that at 100 yards the dot will just cover a circle two inches in diameter. At 200 yards it will cover a four-inch circle, and at 300 yards it will cover a six-inch circle. Similarly, a four-minute dot will cover a four-inch circle at 100 yards and so on. Next the hunter needs to know some dimension on the deer for comparison with the dot. The distance from the shoulders to the bellyline on a big deer is about eighteen inches. On a small deer this distance is about fifteen inches. Say the hunter is using a scope with a three-minute dot. He spots a good-size buck (belly to shoulders estimated as eighteen inches). He uses the dot and finds the shoulder-to-belly distance appears to be two dots high. That means that the dot seems to cover up nine inches, and a three-minute dot covers up nine inches at 300 yards. Thus, the distance to the deer is estimated as 300 yards.

Crosshair reticles designed for rangefinding usually come with a second horizontal crosshair separated from the primary crosshair by a specified number of minutes. The crosshairs are then used to estimate range in the same manner as the dots described above. Weaver scopes use this device. In the Redfield scopes, the distance between the primary and secondary crosshairs is variable. One turns a ring until the crosshairs just bracket the deer from shoulders to belly and then reads the range in the field of view of the scope — no calculations needed.

Range estimation with a post is somewhat more awkward, but it can be done. Flat-top posts have a fixed width at the top. You can get this info from the manufacturer or by taking the scope to a range and seeing how big a circle the post will cover at 100 yards. Assume you determine that the post has a five-minute top. To estimate range, you have to tip the rifle on its side and measure how many post-widths high the deer appears to be from belly to shoulders. If you measure a small deer (fifteen inches from shoulders to belly) as two-post-widths high, that means that the post is covering seven-and-a-half inches. Since the post would cover five inches at 100 yards, the range to the deer is 150 yards.

Mounting the Scope

The hunter looking for a way to mount his scope on his rifle has the choice of two basic mount designs: the bridge, or top, mount and the side mount. Each has its advantages and disadvantages, and the best for you depends on the gun you use, the hunting you plan to do, and personal taste.

Side mounts employ a dovetail device that is fastened to the side of the receiver. The split rings that hold the scope are fastened to a mating female dovetail bar. The stock of most rifles must be in-letted to accept the receiver-mounted plate, and this may be a dis-advantage if you value highly your crotch-grained, hand-rubbed, French walnut stock. It will be an even bigger eyesore if you later remove the side mount and are left with a gaping hole in your gun's woodwork. One advantage of all this unsightly scope-mount-ing hardware is that the side mounts allow the scope to be de-tached quickly and iron sights employed. This cannot be done with the bridge mount, since its base obstructs the iron sights. The side mount also allows the same scope to be used, after rezeroing, on other rifles fitted with the same type of dovetail plate on the re-ceiver. The side mount also does a surprisingly good job of bringing the shot group back to the same point after the scope has been re-moved and returned to the rifle. I checked my Weaver side mount by removing the scope, replacing it, and firing a test group at 100 yards. I did this five times and could detect no shift in the point of impact. Side mounts have a tendency to catch on saddle scabbards and are not as good as top mounts for horseback hunters. If you have a shotgun that you plan to use in the off-season for game other than deer, side mounts are not a bad choice since removal of the scope will allow you to get at the iron sights without removing the top mounts as you would have to with bridge mounts. Some side mounts, such as the Packmayr LoSwing, allow the scope to be swung to the side without detaching it for immediate use of the iron sights. Personally, I like a quick detachable side mount with a receiver peep sight as a backup. Some receiver peep sights, such as the Lyman No. 57, have crossarms that can be removed and re-placed without the use of tools and when replaced maintain their original zero quite well. A deer hunter so equipped who damages his scope simply removes it, drops the crossarm into his receiver-mounted sight base, and is ready to go without having to zero.

Bridge mounts consist of two dovetailed bases or a dove-tailed base bar that screws on to the receiver bridge and the re-ceiver ring. Two split rings with mating dovetails are secured to the scope. Such mounts are very sturdy and allow a scope to be switched from rifle to rifle after rezeroing or allow different scopes to be used on a given gun. The major drawback of the top mounts is that most of them obstruct the iron sights even when the scope is removed. There are, however, some exceptions. The Weaver Pivot Mount is a top mount that permits the scope to be swung out of the way of the iron sights. But arrangements such as this preclude the use of receiver peep sights unless the hunter is willing to remove the peep sight crossarm as described above when the peep sight is not in use. These swinging, quick-switch, glass-to-iron arrange-ments are designed for use with open iron sights.

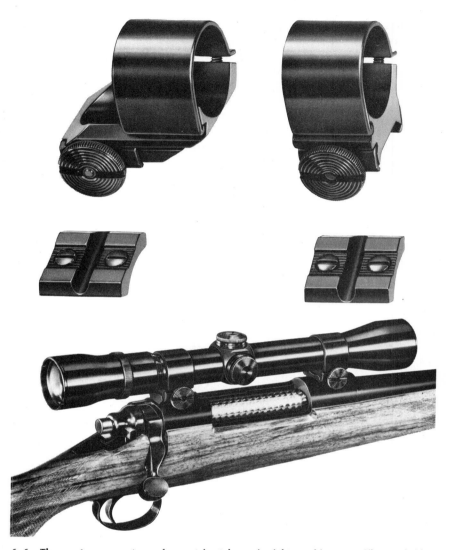

6-6 The most common type of mount for telescopic sights on big-game rifles are bridge mounts. The upper photo shows the dovetail base plates that are permanently mounted on the rifle and the split rings that secure the scope to the base plates. The lower photo shows the mounting hardware as it would actually be installed on a rifle. (Courtesy of Weaver)

In addition to mounts, such as the Weaver Pivot mount, that allow the hunter to swing the scope out of the way, there are other designs meant to accommodate both iron and telescopic sights. For example, the Williams Quick Convertible mount allows the scope to be unscrewed from the base mount and a rear aperture to be screwed into the base. The entire conversion process from glass to iron or vice versa takes about one minute. In the case of swing mounts such as the Weaver, the conversion takes less than five seconds. Another scheme meant to accommodate both iron and telescopic sights is a top mount that holds the scope high enough over the barrel for the shooter to sight through the sights under the telescopic sight. An example of this type of mount is the Redfield See-Thru. The major drawback of this type of mount is that its scope is mounted too high for firm placement of the cheek against the stock. Alternatively, if the stock is shaped to align with the high scope, it is misaligned for the lower iron sights.

6-7 A Weaver K3 scope is shown at left and above mounted on a Winchester Model 70 rifle by means of Weaver Pivot Mounts. The left photo shows the scope in the normal aiming position. In the above photo, the scope has been swung to the side to make the iron sights available. This type of mount makes for quick and easy conversion from scope to iron sights, and when the scope is swung back again it returns surprisingly close to its original point of aim. (Courtesy of Weaver)

There are other important points to consider in the selection and use of a scope. When mounting the scope, be sure to mount it far enough forward to avoid the scope's slamming into your eye when the gun recoils. This means a minimum of three to three-and-a-half inches between the rear of the scope and your face. For years I had seen men walking around rifle ranges with big shiners or cuts

6-8 It is now possible to mount a scope on the famous Model 94 Winchester. In the past, this most popular deer rifle presented a problem to the hunter who wanted to mount a scope, because the spent cases are ejected out the top of the receiver. Special mounts are now available that mount the scope in front of the receiver, and low-power scopes with long eye reliefs are used. The scope shown here is a Bushnell 2.5x Phantom. (Courtesy of Bushnell)

around their eyes from being hit with recoiling scopes. I always wondered how anyone could be so foolish—until it happened to me. I was sitting high on a rocky ledge one chilly November afternoon watching one of my favorite deer runs. Sure enough, just before dusk, a bit fat spikehorn came ambling down the trail like it was Sunset Boulevard. So I raised my rifle and picked up a nice sight picture. There was only one problem. I was sitting in an awkward position and was unable to plant the butt of the rifle firmly against my shoulder. When I squeezed that round off, my .30/06 recoiled a good six inches. The scope eventually encountered a solid object, my head, and came to rest. When I got that deer gutted, there was more of my own blood on me than there was of his.

A handy piece of accessory gear for the scope hunter is a set of lens covers. Lens covers will protect your scope lenses from marks and scratches and will help keep rain and fog from fouling up your scope. If you get scope covers, get the transparent ones. In an emergency, you can look through them without having to delay and take them off. One suggestion though: don't walk off and forget your lens covers at your stand as so many hunters do. I have found more than one set of lens covers in the woods forgotten there by some hunter who laid them down next to him instead of putting them in his pocket.

There was a time when I felt that it was absolutely essential to have iron sights as backup for a scope. I don't think so anymore. I have used scopes for years and only once did I have a scope go out of commission on me, and that was my own fault. I got caught out in a wet snow with my lens covers nice and safe and dry in the trunk of my car. The hunter who goes on long hikes or pack trips should have iron sights as a backup. He's in deep trouble a twenty-mile horseback ride from nowhere when his partner drops a heavy saddle bag on his scope and demolishes it. But most hunters could go through a lifetime of hunting with little or no inconvenience using just a scope with good strong top mounts.

7

Handguns, Bows,
and Black Powder

It may surprise many whitetail hunters to know that there are some people who find bagging a deer so easy that they feel there is no challenge to it. It has been my experience that such folk usually owe their success to having the good fortune to hunt in areas of good range with light hunting pressure. Often they hunt on private land. Whatever the reason for the ease with which they collect their venison, there are two ways to reinstate the challenge of the hunt. One way is to hunt only for trophies. A hunter who sets as a goal collecting a rack that will land him in Boone and Crockett's top ten will find no end of challenge, no matter where he hunts.

The other way to reintroduce challenge into the hunt is to switch to handguns or primitive weapons. Hunting with these weapons requires that the hunter hone his woodcraft to a sharp edge, and short of going afield with a pocket full of large rocks, hunting whitetail deer with these weapons provides the greatest possible hunting challenge.

Handguns

Some shooting pundits claim that the handgun has no business in the deer woods. I disagree. I think that some handguns and some handgunners have no business in the deer woods, but that's a different story; some rifles and some rifle hunters have no business in the woods either. Modern high-power handguns employed by disciplined shooters are effective deer takers.

What constitutes an adequate handgun for deer? At this point it is necessary to recall the comments in Chapter 4 concerning what constitutes sportsmanlike hunting. If you can humanely and consistently bring down the game at which you shoot, then you are adequately armed. If you can't, then you better move up to something more powerful or engage in a little more marksmanship practice. Hunters who choose to go afield with less powerful weapons voluntarily assume the burden of more accurate shot placement.

The only two handgun calibers I would call adequate for deer in factory loadings are the .41 Remington Magnum and the .44 Remington Magnum. The .357 Magnum fans will no doubt protest that their cartridge is more than adequate for deer. After all, it pushes the 150-grain bullet out the business end of an 8⅜-inch barrel with 845 foot-pounds of energy. This is a big hatful of energy when one compares it to most other handgun cartridges. But I consider this a little on the shy side for deer. The venerable old .30/30, which most agree is on the light side of the spectrum of deer-hunting rifles, has more energy at 200 yards than the .357 Magnum has at the muzzle. And I wouldn't recommend the use of a .30/30 on deer at 200 yards.

The .41 Remington Magnum and the .44 Remington Magnum are in reality hand-held howitzers. The .41 Remington Magnum dishes out about 25 percent less recoil than its big brother, but neither is meant for women, small boys, or the faint of heart. Both handle less potent cartridges for target practice. The .41 Remington Magnum comes factory loaded in a mild (?) version that only turns up 515 foot-pounds at the muzzle as opposed to the full load's 1,050 foot-pounds. The .44 Remington Magnum accepts the .44 Special loads which, at 311 foot-pounds of muzzle energy, provide

7-1 The Smith & Wesson Model 57 comes chambered for the potent .41 Remington Magnum and is an effective deer getter. (Courtesy of Smith & Wesson)

a welcome relief from the full load's 1,150 foot-pounds. Pertinent ballistic data on these two cartridges is as follows:

CARTRIDGE	BARREL LENGTH	BULLET WEIGHT	BULLET TYPE	MUZZLE ENERGY	ENERGY AT 100 YARDS
.41 RM	8 ¾	210	Soft Point	1,050	650
.44 RM	6 ½	240	Soft Point	1,150	750

In the hands of a shooter who is willing to discipline himself and take only sure shots, either cartridge should be effective on deer to at least fifty or sixty yards.

Handguns for these heavy cartridges should have custom-fitted grips and a rear sight adjustable for windage and elevation. Some gunners prefer a scope of one to one-and-a-half power. The scope makes the gun a little harder to carry and requires a special holster, but it does make sighting easier. Barrel length should be long enough to carry around without tripping over it. The added barrel length improves accuracy and greatly increases muzzle energy. In the short-barrelled handguns, the gases are still expanding when the bullet leaves the muzzle, so the bullet does not get maximum push. The same Remington .44 Magnum that delivers 1,150 foot-pounds of muzzle energy from the 6½-inch barrel of a pistol provides 1,750 foot-pounds from a twenty-two-inch rifle.

There are several high-quality revolvers chambered for the .41 and .44 Remington Magnums. The Smith & Wesson Model 57 comes in .41 Remington Magnum, and the Model 29 is chambered for .44 Remington Magnum. Choose the 8⅜-inch barrel in either model. For fanciers of single-action revolvers, the Rugers are available in these big calibers. The Ruger New Model Blackhawk has a 6½-inch barrel and is available in .41 Remington Magnum, while the New Model Super Blackhawk has a 7½-barrel and is chambered for the more potent .44 Remington Magnum.

Bows

The last twenty years have seen a tremendous increase in the popularity of archery. While target-shooting clubs and associations have increased their enrollment during this period, most of the credit for archery's new-found popularity must be given to bow hunting.

The bow is a weapon of ancient man and has long been used for hunting and warfare. In the Middle Ages, the bow gained ascendancy as the deadliest of man's battlefield weapons. The first real hint of the bow's effectiveness came on a bright autumn day at a spot between London and Hastings, England. The date was October 14, 1066. Here it was that Harold Godwinson, the newly selected king of England chose to defend a ridge line with 11,000 troops against a roughly equal number of invading Frenchman commanded by William, Duke of Normandy. In four successive assaults, each preceded by a withering rain of arrows, the French forces routed the English. William the Bastard became William the Conqueror, and the bow became the prime battlefield weapon of Europe.

This military experience was by no means lost on the British. By the beginning of the fourteenth century, the English had developed what amounted to a national weapon. It was a weapon that was to reign supreme on the battlefield until the advent of gunpowder — the longbow. In the hands of a trained yeoman the longbow was remarkably accurate; in fact, the normal tournament range with this bow was 220 yards, and it was capable of firing an arrow twice that far. The longbow was superior in range and firepower to the crossbow, and for 200 years it gave the English armies a decided advantage on the battlefield.

With the adoption of portable firearms by European armies in the late fifteenth and early sixteenth centuries, the bow, sword, and spear rapidly declined in military importance. Even the use of bows as sporting devices lay dormant for many years. Interest in archery in this country was rekindled by the publication in 1877 of a collection of writings by Maurice Thompson entitled *The Witchery of Archery*. Maurice and his brother Will had fought for the Confederacy in the Civil War, and the end of hostilities found them with no means of making a living. Maurice had been wounded in the War, and doctors recommended an outdoor life for him. As ex-Confederates, both Will and Maurice were forbidden to carry firearms. So they turned to archery. They lived in the wilds, hunted game, made their own equipment, and singlehandedly revived interest in archery. Their marksmanship feats are legendary, and Will was five times national champion.

7-2 Besides being enjoyable and challenging, bow hunting can be highly productive, as demonstrated by these two successful hunters. (Courtesy of Bear Archery)

The modern-day bow hunting revival can be attributed to another pair of bow-hunting partners, Dr. Saxton Pope and Arthur Young. Pope and Young acknowledged their debt to the Thompson brothers, and they were also influenced greatly by a colorful hunting partnership with Ishi, the last of the Yana Indians of California. From 1911 till his death in 1916, Ishi was the hunting and shooting companion of Pope and Young. He greatly influenced them with his Indian hunting methods. Dr. Pope's 1923 volume, *Hunting with the Bow and Arrow,* has had much the same effect in this century as the Thompson book had nearly a half century earlier. In 1934, Wisconsin became the first state to hold a special deer season for bow hunters, and today every state in the union has a special season or special areas for bow hunters for at least some types of game.

Today's bow hunter is given a choice of two general types of bows, the simple bow and the compound bow, both of which are vastly superior to anything that was available in the days of Pope

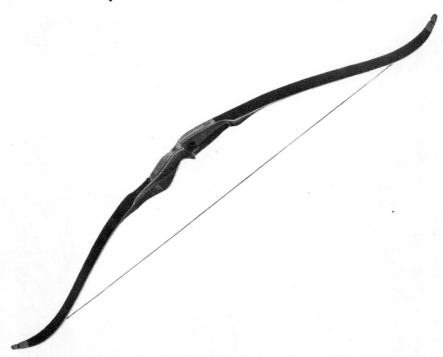

7–3   Typical simple bow intended for hunters. (Courtesy of Bear Archery)

and Young. The simple bow has a one-piece bowstring that runs straight from one tip to the other when the bow is braced (strung). The compound bow is a complex system of string or wire, pulleys, and adjusting devices intended to give the archer a mechanical advantage and to make it easier to draw the bow. As far as the simple bow is concerned, modern technology has produced a durable and beautiful bow that is capable of shooting arrows straighter and further and with less effort than earlier designs. The most common design for today's simple hunting bow is the recurve design of the Turks and Persians. Like the Turkish bows, modern recurve bows are laminates, but today fiberglass is laminated over the wood instead of the sinew laminate that was used on the Turkish weapons.

Compound bows are the most startling and impressive innovation in bow technology since the invention of the longbow. With a simple bow, the archer is holding the arrow and bowstring back at full draw against the maximum pull of the bow. With a compound bow, however, the bow goes through its point of maximum pull at some point before full draw, and then as the arrow is drawn back further the bow relaxes or "lets off," and at full draw

7-4   Typical compound bow intended for hunters. (Courtesy of Bear Archery)

the archer may be holding back as little as 50 percent of the maximum pull of the bow.

For the hunter used to shooting a simple bow, his first encounter with a compound is bound to be a revelation. I recall the first time I drew back a compound bow. The bow was a 50-pound Bear. I drew it back through its point of maximum pull, and as I drew it back further it started to let off. The let-off was so impressive and so dramatic that I nearly dropped the thing in fright. I was sure that some yield point or breaking stress had been exceeded and that I was about to be strangled and impaled in an explosion of wood and fiberglass splinters, wire, string, and pulleys.

Some bow-hunting purists regard compounds as "contraptions" that have no place in the arsenal of a serious bowhunter. Others, more pragmatic, claim that there is no sense in disregarding technological and design improvements. Which of these views you subscribe to depends on what you want to get from your bow hunting. If you are looking for a more primitive weapon, more in keeping with the tradition of the American Indian and the English long-bowmen, you will probably want a simple bow. If, on the other hand, you are after the most efficient game getter and the one that is most easily mastered, you will probably select a compound bow. In defense of the compound-bow hunter, I would point out that he is, in my opinion, using a weapon more primitive and more difficult to master than either the handgunner or the black-powder shooter, and the latter are in turn at a disadvantage compared to the smokeless-powder rifle or shotgun hunter. In addition, it should be noted that the simple-bow advocates who are bemoaning and belittling the newfangled compound bow are in most cases carrying highly sophisticated bows and arrows made in part of plastic, fiberglass, aluminum, nylon, and other products of modern technology. Certainly these bows are also a far cry from the primitive weapons of the Indian. There are some bow hunters who feel than an honest hunting bow should be completely homemade out of natural materials personally collected by the archer. This latter camp feels that all the simple-bow hunters with their "store boughten" bows made of "plastic" are a bunch of frauds. It all boils down to what you want to get out of your bow-hunting experience.

Deer hunters generally choose bows in the four-foot to five-foot lengths because the shorter bows are easier to maneuver through brush and in tight places like tree stands. In addition to length, the prospective bow hunter must know what weight bow he wants. The weight of a bow is the force in pounds required to bring the bow to a twenty-eight-inch draw. While simple bow weights from sixty to seventy pounds were once common among deer hunters, design improvements have made modern bows in the forty-five-to-fifty-five-pound range quite adequate for deer. One of the worst mistakes that a hunter can make is to select a bow that is too heavy. He will have difficulty drawing the bow to full draw, find it impossible to hold steady, will tire too quickly, and will develop bad shooting habits. A good rule of thumb for a simple bow is to determine the weight you can hold steadily at full draw for ten seconds and then choose a bow five to ten pounds heavier. You will grow into the heavier weight quickly with shooting practice.

For a compound bow I like to wind up with a let-off weight in the thirty-five-to-forty-pound range. A sixty-pound bow with a 40 percent let-off will have a full draw pull (weight) of thirty-six pounds. Bows in this range are fairly comfortable for me, and maximum weights of up to seventy pounds I find I can handle. Anything over that gets fairly tiring on the target range, and I don't really think that such heavy weights are necessary for deer. Certainly the heavier bows will shoot flatter and be effective at longer ranges (if you are an accurate shot), but I would be inclined to recommend for deer hunting a compound bow in the fifty-to-sixty-five-pound class with a let-off from 30 to 40 percent. Too much let-off makes it difficult to accurately match arrow spine, which is discussed later, to the weight of the bow.

Arrows

As important as selection of a hunting bow is, selection of the arrows is even more important. It is the arrow that must fly true from the bow to the target, and it is the arrow that must do the killing job quickly and humanely.

Hunting arrows are usually made of wood, fiberglass, or aluminum. Wooden arrows are the cheapest, but are the most easily broken and are more likely to take a set or curve if improperly stored. Fiberglass arrows are intermediate in price between wood and aluminum. Fiberglass arrows are tough, will take a lot of abuse, and can be bent almost to breaking and still retain their straightness. Alumnium arrows are the most accurate and most expensive.

The arrows that you select must be matched in stiffness to your bow. Arrows that are longer than you need are unnecessarily heavy and hence have a more arched trajectory. If the arrow is too short you might accidentally draw it back beyond the bow, which could result in shooting yourself in the hand. There are several ways to determine the correct arrow length for you. One way is to hold your arms outstretched in front of you, palms together and fingers extended. With the nock of the arrow against your chest, the tip should just reach your fingertips. Another way to determine arrow length is to measure the fingertip-to-fingertip distance of your outstretched arms. Knowing this distance, use the following table to determine correct arrow length.

ARM SPAN (INCHES)	ARROW LENGTH (INCHES)
63–65	24–25
66–68	25–26
69–71	26–27
72–74	27–28
75–77	28–29
Over 77	30–32

Shooting arrows longer or shorter than twenty-eight inches will result in a change in the effective weight of your bow since bow weights are measured by the manufacturer at twenty-eight-inch draw. The change in weight is about two-and-a-half pounds per inch of draw change. Thus a forty-five-pound bow will have a weight of somewhere around fifty pounds when drawn full with thirty-inch arrows.

When the archer releases his bowstring, the arrow does not leap instantly from the bow. Under the strong force of the bowstring, the arrow buckles or curves initially before it gets moving. The amount of curvature must be exact if the arrow is to fly smoothly past the bow. Once again, modern bow design comes to the hunters' rescue. In older bows, the arrow rest was not deeply inletted into the side of the bow. As the arrow flexed under the compressive force of the bowstring, it had to arch in order to get safely around the entire thickness of the bow handle. Modern materials and design allow the arrow rest to be inletted so far into the handle riser that the arrow is nearly centered in the riser and does not have to "get around" so much of the bow on its way to the target. As a result, modern arrows do not have to be matched in stiffness, or spine as archers call it, nearly as closely as their more primitive predecessors.

In spite of this quality of modern bows, the hunter should make certain the spine of the arrow he buys is matched as closely as possible to his bow. This is done by specifying the length of the arrows and the weight of the bow. For compound bows, some archers take the average of the maximum draw weight of the bow and the let-off weight when specifying spine. For example, for a sixty-pound bow with a let-off weight of thirty-six pounds the archer would specify a bow weight of forty-eight pounds (sixty plus thirty-six divided by two). I personally prefer stiffer arrows and always specify maximum draw weight, in this case sixty pounds, for compounds. By providing draw-weight information, the archer is telling the manufacturer the force to which the arrow will be subjected and, therefore, how much spine it must have.

Once the length and the spine have been determined, the arrowhead itself must be selected. For actual shooting at game, the deer hunter will want some type of broadhead. Broadheads come with either two, three, or four cutting edges. Since the arrow kills by causing hemorrhaging rather than by shock as a rifle bullet does, I have always preferred four-edge broadheads like the Bear Razorhead and the Herter Magnum. For target practice, get a set of target arrows matched in length and spine to your hunting arrows. Some companies offer broadhead tips that screw off and can be replaced with specially weighted target tips meant to duplicate the flight of the broadheads. These arrows make handy hunting–target practice combinations, and the small aerodynamic difference between the target and broadhead tip is not great enough to disturb the average hunter.

Discussing arrow color is like discussing sex, politics, or religion. Everyone goes into such a discussion with a fixed opinion and comes out of the discussion with the same fixed opinion in spite of all the verbal exchanges. Therefore I will simply state both sides of the case and you can be your own judge. First, there is the school of supersleuths who believe that arrow shafts and fletchings should be camouflaged, or at least brown or green, to prevent the quarry from seeing the approaching hunter. These are the guys who go around so camouflaged that they keep bumping into each other in camp because they can't see one another.

Then there are the good guys with snow-white arrow shafts. They claim that the white shafts are easier to see en route to the target, and if the shot is a miss the next shot is more readily corrected if you saw where the first shot went. Furthermore, arrows that miss or go through the target are easier to find under most woodland and target conditions if the shafts are white. (Obviously this is not so if you plan to do much hunting in the snow.) These hunters claim that the white shafts are not a giveaway if the hunter is in a blind or is moving as slowly as he should be. I would like to go on record as coming down firmly and unequivocably on this issue—right in the middle. I use bright yellow shafts.

Archery Accessories

There are a number of accessory items that are indispensible to the bow hunter. The first and most obvious is an extra bowstring matched in length to the one on his bow. A badly frayed or broken bowstring can put a quick end to an otherwise well-planned hunting trip. The next accessory item that the bowhunter will need is an armguard. This device is worn on the forearm of the arm that holds the bow. If a short-sleeve shirt is worn, the armguard will protect the forearm from a painful slap by the bowstring. If a loose garment is worn, it will keep the sleeve from interfering with the forward travel of the bowstring. A flat file is another must item for the bow hunter's accessory bag. Broadheads must be kept razor sharp at all times; and in addition to filing, a light coat of WD-40 or a silicon spray is useful to prevent rusting. I have also found the cord bow-stringer to be a great help. Many a good hunting bow has been ruined by improper use of the step-through method of bow-stringing with a resultant twisted bow limb. A cord bow-stringer makes it possible even for a woman to easily string a forty-five-pound or fifty-five-pound bow.

For the rifleman, carrying a few extra rounds is no big problem. A few three-inch-long cartridges can be thrown into a pocket (or better yet, one in each pocket so they don't rattle). Two-and-a-half-foot-long arrows are a different story. Archers over the years have developed and experimented with a great variety of quivers. Back and shoulder quivers are adequate for the target shooter and for certain open terrain hunting at small game. But for deer hunters, this type of quiver is not a good choice. It is noisy and the arrows catch on every low-hanging limb. I have found the most convenient quivers to be the so-called bow quivers. This quiver attaches to the bow on the side opposite the arrow rest and will carry three to eight arrows. The better bow quivers have a hood that covers the broad-heads to prevent injury should the archer fall and to prevent dul-ling of the broadhead's cutting edges by brushing against limbs and branches.

To protect the fingertips in contact with the bowstring and to help insure a smooth release, archers wear a shooting glove or a shooting tab. Some tabs are just short tubes of leather that slip over the fingers. Others have the tubes of leather connected to a strap around the wrist. Probably the most useful for the bow hunter is the full glove or the glove with cutaway back. The gloves are less likely to become lost and are more likely to be in place when the times comes for a shot.

Most bow hunters find bow sights helpful. Sights are avail-able in varying degrees of sophistication and some have both wind-age and elevation adjustments. Bow sights have two big advantages aside from the fact that they make it easier for most people to ob-tain a good sight picture. In the first place, bow sights help correct certain shooting faults, such as canting the bow. Secondly, they help overcome the big mental mistake that many bow hunters make of shooting at the whole deer rather than selecting a small vital area and aiming specifically at it. For some reason, partly connected with buck fever and partly attributable to the fact that a bow with-out a sight doesn't have a crosshair to lay neatly on the target, a dis-tressingly large number of bow-hunters will see a deer and then loose an arrow in that general direction completely forgetting their slow and deliberate practice shots. A bow sight can help correct this gross fault. One of the major drawbacks of a bowsight is that it is fragile and easily broken. Spare parts should be carried.

Bow-hunting Ethics

Rifle hunters sometimes question the ethics of hunting deer with a bow since a bow has less "muzzle energy" than a .38 Special. And most sane folk would agree that a .38 Special is too little gun for deer. The answer, of course, is that the broadhead and the bullet kill by different means. The high-velocity bullet kills with shock, whereas the razor-sharp broadhead causes massive hemorrhaging.

I do believe, however, that the rifle hunters have a point. Af-ter years of discussing hunt results with bowmen, I am convinced that bow hunters leave more cripples in the woods per deer taken than gun hunters do. I have had a disturbingly large number of bow hunters make remarks to me like, "Got six shots off last year, but didn't get my deer. Gonna do better this year." Assuming the indi-vidual who made this remark was such a lousy shot that he completely missed three times, he still left three cripples. There are, I think, several reasons for this poor showing on the part of many bow hunters, and none of the reasons is attributable to any inherent shortcoming of the bow. For one thing, most bow hunters don't practice enough. The average man, with one afternoon of instruction and practice, can become a good enough rifle shot to consistently keep his shots in the magic twelve-inch circle at 100 yards. Not so with a bow. Bow-shooting proficiency comes only with many afternoons of practice over many months. The bowman who thinks he is ready because he groups in a twelve-inch circle at forty yards on a practice range after he's been warming up for an hour is kidding himself. The question to ask is: can this same archer walk out of his house cold, stalk around the woods for an hour, and then place his first arrow in the twelve-inch circle at some unknown distance between fifteen and forty yards? Or will the first shot be a foot to the right resulting in a paunch-shot cripple?

Another reason for bow-hunting cripples is the difficulty of getting within bow range. After a long and exasperating day of stalking without getting close to a deer, the hunter is tempted by long shots or shots through brush. This is asking for a wounded animal. Again we get back to the old question of shot discipline. Earlier I called on the gun hunters to get from 90 to 95 percent of the deer at which they shoot. Because of the inherent difficulty of bow hunting, I am not sure that this is feasible for the archer. I would like to think that it is, but each man must let his own conscience be his guide.

Bow-hunting Technique

I will dispatch the subject of bow-hunting technique quickly, because I don't think there is any such thing. There are hunting techniques or methods, such as driving or stalking, and they apply equally to gun hunters and to bowhunters. It is true that the bow hunter must refine these techniques to a higher degree than the gun hunter, but the basic methods are the same. The bow hunter may have to resort to such trickery as using camouflaged clothing and scents to hide his human scent, but this is not because his stalking is any different from the gun hunter's stalking. The bow hunter just has to get closer. In fact, one of the big advantages of bow hunting is that it teaches the hunter many lessons that can be carried over to the gun season. Many a case-hardened gun enthusiast with fixed ways has been forced to start learning all over again when he took up bow hunting.

Black Powder

The last ten years have seen a resurgence in the popularity of black-powder shooting. This revival of interest has been spurred by the Civil War centennial, the nation's Bicentennial, and the provisions by many states of special seasons for the black-powder hunter similar to the special seasons for bow hunters. The nostalgia factor and the beauty of the guns themselves cannot be denied as additional contributing factors in this new-found popularity. The shooter and hunter can now select from a wide variety of well-made and beautiful guns available from a number of domestic distributors. When not being carried afield, many of these modern reproductions make excellent wall trappings and will do much to spruce up a drab den wall. The black-powder guns which are undergoing the interest revival are the muzzle-loading reproductions and replicas (as opposed to breech-loaders). While both long arms and handguns are enjoying this renewed interest, the following discussion will concentrate on rifles and muskets since I do not consider black-powder handguns to be satisfactory deer slayers.

There are two types of muzzle-loader available to the black-powder enthusiast today: the flintlock and the caplock. The difference is the system used to ignite the powder charge. The flintlock was invented early in the seventeenth century and was a big improvement over earlier ignition systems. It was gradually replaced in the early 1800s by the more reliable caplock, which remained the favored ignition system until it in turn was replaced by the breech-loader.

7–5   This "Kentucky" rifle is available from its importer, Century Arms, in either flintlock or caplock. The upper rifle is the flintlock, the lower the caplock. Note the difference in the ignition systems. (Courtesy Century Arms)

The flintlock ignition consists of a powder pan, a frizzen, and a hammer that has locked in its jaws a piece of flint. The hammer is first cocked. When the trigger is pulled, the hammer falls forward and the flint strikes the spring-loaded frizzen. As the frizzen moves forward and upward, the abrasive impact of the flint on the hardened-steel frizzen sends a shower of sparks down into the powder pan where they ignite the priming charge. When the priming charge ignites, it sends a flame through a small hole in the barrel into the powder charge behind the projectile. There results a thunderous roar, a billowing belch of smoke, and a magnificent tongue of fire that is truly a joy to behold. With a good breeze blowing, the smoke will soon clear; and shortly thereafter one can survey the damage that the mighty thunderstick has wrought upon the surrounding countryside.

The caplock system also has a small hole penetrating through the end of the barrel into the powder-charge space. However, the caplock system has a projection or nipple that sticks out about one half inch from the barrel and the hole goes through this nipple into the barrel. To fire the gun, the shooter simply places the open end of an ignition cap, which contains a solidified priming charge, over the end of the nipple and pulls the trigger after first cocking the hammer. The hammer falls forward, strikes the cap, and detonates the priming charge. The priming charge flashes down the hole in the nipple and ignites the main charge behind the projectile. The result is spectacular explosion similar to that from the flintlock.

As far as reliability and efficiency are concerned, the caplock is a far superior ignition system. The flintlock may have its priming powder blown out of the pan or moistened in the pan and thus not firing. (Hence the expression "Keep your powder dry.") The flintlock is also more susceptible to having the priming charge fail to propagate through the touch hole and thus failing to ignite the main charge. The result is a lot of smoky activity in the pan but no discharge. (Hence the expression "Flash in the pan.") Another advantage of the caplock over the flintlock is that the caplock has a much shorter delay time from the instant the trigger is pulled until the weapon fires. With the flintlock, the shooter has to hold his sight picture for the eternity during which the hammer is falling, the sparks are flying, and the priming charge is flashing. Holding a steady aim while all these fireworks are going on a few inches in front of one's face takes a fair amount of practice. In view of all these disadvantages, why would anyone select a flintlock rifle over a caplock? For the same reasons that one would select a muzzle-loader over the more efficient modern weapons. The challenge is greater and the weapon is more primitive. It is difficult to imagine the spirits of Davy Crockett and Daniel Boone stalking along by your side when you are armed with a Remington Model 700C Custom Magnum with variable scope. But with a fine old Brown Bess or Kentucky flintlock in hand—that's a different story!

So the choice of a black-powder gun is up to you. As with

the choice between simple and compound bows, it depends on what you want to get out of your hunting experience. If you prefer the flintlocks, you can choose from such weapons as the Hopkins and Allen Minuteman, Dixie Gun Works' Brown Bess, and Navy Arms' Kentucky Flintlock. Many of these guns are imported by several companies and you may want to shop around. Quality seems to vary somewhat from importer to importer, and if you are a fanatic about wood-to-metal fits and other such details, you will probably want to inspect the guns in person and compare.

There is a larger selection of caplocks. If you like the replica or traditional styles, possibilities include High Standard's Pennsylvania Long Rifle, Intercontinental Arms' Kentucky Rifle, and Navy Arms' Zouave Percussion carbine. Many of these guns come in a choice of either flintlock or percussion (caplock), and if you are a do-it-yourselfer, a number of them are available in kit form at a considerable savings. If you are less interested in tradition and more concerned with having an efficient hunting arm, you might be interested in a gun such as the Harrington & Richardson Huntsman Percussion rifle. In addition to its more modern lines, this gun has a rear sight adjustable for windage and elevation. Several standard and widely available reference books, such as *Gun Digest,* give comprehensive compilations of the currently available black-powder guns and the prospective purchaser would do well to start his purchase selection by referring to such a listing.

Another factor to consider in selecting a black-powder gun for deer hunting is your state's hunting laws. Some states place a caliber restriction on black-powder weapons. In Ohio, for example, black-powder guns used for deer hunting must be at least .38 caliber. In addition, if the guns are to be used during a special primitive-weapons season, many states have additional restrictions. Typical restrictions are that it must be a muzzle-loader, it must be single shot, and it may not be equipped with telescopic sights. Check your local game laws since some of these restrictions may not apply in your area and others may. If you are not a traditionalist and are simply looking for the most effective black-powder weapon, a low-power scope can be helpful even on a charcoal burner. If you plan to mount a scope, you should consider the Hopkins and Allen Deer Stalker from High Standard since this gun employs a bottom-mounted ignition system that will not interfere with a scope.

Black-powder guns usable for deer hunting fire two types of projectiles: round balls and Minié balls. Round balls, as the name implies, are spheres of soft lead. After pouring the powder charge into the muzzle, the shooter places a patch of cloth over the muzzle, sets the ball on the patch, and taps the ball part way into

7–6 Rifle, powder flask, Minié balls, and caps. The makings of a pleasant afternoon of black-powder shooting.

the muzzle. He then trims away the excess patch material and drives the ball home with the ramrod. The patch serves to seal the space between the barrel walls and the ball and thereby prevents gasses from escaping around the ball.

The Minié ball is shaped more like a conventional bullet. No patch is used when firing a Minié ball since the gas seal is provided by deformation of the ball and an increase in its diameter under the force of the expanding gases. Either projectile is satisfactory for deer hunting, and you should start with the manufacturer's recommendation for your gun and if so inclined experiment from there. Certain guns and certain rifling twists handle one type or weight of projectile better than another.

As with any deer-hunting weapon, it is imperative that the hunter fully understands that the capabilities of his black-powder gun include its ballistics. Consider, for example, the .58 caliber Buffalo Hunter percussion rifle with a 25 ½-inch barrel. This is one of my favorites for deer because of its short barrel and easy portability. If I load in 100 grains of FFg propellant (a fairly standard black-powder granulation) behind a 570-grain Minié ball, the projectile will come barrelling out of the muzzle with approximately 1,450 foot-pounds of energy. At 100 yards it will retain 1,100 foot-pounds; and at 200 yards, about 890 foot-pounds. The drop at 100 yards is ten inches, and at 200 yards it is about sixty inches. If the gun is zeroed at 100 yards the midrange trajectory is four-and-a-half inches. Zeroed at 100 yards, the gun is an effective deer killer with this charge-and-projectile combination out to about 150 yards. At this point the residual energy slips under 1,000 foot pounds, and the drop becomes difficult to estimate.

Until recently, it was difficult for shooters to get reliable and complete data on black-powder ballistics. Black-powder projectile ballistics are dependent on powder charge, projectile type, and barrel length; there are so many combinations possible that extensive tables would be needed to tabulate adequately the ballistics of all, or even the most popular, combinations. Lyman has come to the shooter's rescue with the publication of their *Black Powder Handbook*. This handbook is a gold mine of information for the black-powder enthusiast. It is chock-full of ballistic tables from which you can either read or closely approximate the ballistic performance of your muzzle-loading thunderstick. The book also gives lots of useful information on the techniques of shooting both Minié balls and patched round balls. Once you have an idea of the ballistics of your gun, load, and projectile combination, the next step is to go to the range and practice with your gun until you are thoroughly familiar and comfortable with it. This is particularly true of flintlocks, which require a somewhat different discipline to shoot.

The shooter, then, who opts to accept the challenge of black-powder hunting has a good selection of guns from which to choose. These guns are less effective than modern high-powered rifles, but in the hands of an experienced and disciplined hunter they are lethal and capable of humane one-shot kills. Kills tend to be fewer and farther between, but the rewards somehow seem to be proportionally greater. And then there's Davy Crockett and Dan'l Boone who will be stalking along with you.

8

Clothing and Other Equipment

Most deer hunters somehow or other manage to select an adequate rifle for their purposes. Maybe it's because of good advice from hunting friends, or maybe the proprietor of the local gun store sets them straight. But the good advice seems to run out when it comes to suggestions on clothing and other accessories. Maybe this is because the hunter's friends are also improperly dressed and the gun store owner never sets foot in the woods when the temperature is below 70 degrees.

Clothing

Aside from carrying a decent rifle instead of a slingshot, the biggest favor that a hunter can do for himself to insure a successful hunt is to dress properly. The woods are full of deer that owe their old-age pensions to the fidgeting movements of a cold and uncomfortable hunter. Dress in the warmer climates and during the warmer part of the northern deer seasons does not seem to present much of a problem. But most hunters seem to run into problems when the mercury starts to drop.

The place to begin dressing warm is right against your skin. I like two-piece woolen long johns over regular cotton underwear. For really bitter cold, quilted thermal underwear is best. It provides extra insulation with little extra weight. The disadvantage of this underwear is it is bulky and takes longer to dry out should you somehow manage to get drenched. The long johns are probably a better choice in most areas.

For fairly open woods hunting, woolen trousers are tough to beat. They hold up well, provide good insulation, and are comfortable. Very thick brush and brambles, however, tend to tatter and shred the wool, whereas denim blue jeans do a good job of resisting the tears and pulls of brambles. The denims, if at all loose fitting, have a tendency to swish when the hunter walks. Therefore, a fairly form-fitting cut, such as Levis, should be selected. Wool, on the other hand, is soft and quiet, and this is a big consideration for the hunter who likes to stalk his game. Neither wool nor denim will stand up to the cactus, sotol, lechuguilla, and creosote bushes of the Southwest, and the hunter planning to hunt in these areas may need leather-fronted jeans or chaps, especially if he is hunting or doing much traveling on horseback.

Wool is also a good material for shirts and coats. If the shirt is to be worn as an outer garment, state law in many places requires that it be red or orange. Shirt size must be selected with the idea in mind that even with extra underwear you do not want to lose your freedom of movement.

Red wool hunting coats are practical. They have all the usual virtues of wool, comply with state laws on colors, and have more pockets than a pool hall. Get one with a removable hood or have a hood made for it and put the hood in the game pocket in the back of the coat. The hood gets in the way when you don't need it, but on a cold blustery day when you've been on stand for two hours, it's a lifesaver. In very thick or brambly countryside, give some consideration again to blue denim. Denim jackets have long been a favorite with western horseback hunters who found that these jackets stand up well to abrasion from brush.

8-1 Wool is one of the best choices of material for hunting clothing in cool and cold climates. It is quiet, warm, and wears well.

The difference between good and poor footgear is also the difference between enjoyable and miserable hunts. It is an often overlooked truism that the footgear selected has to be custom-fitted to the terrain, weather, and type of hunting as well as the hunter. While walking comfort may be of paramount importance to a drive hunter, warmth is more important to a stand hunter.

In fairly warm climates, if the hunter is planning to stalk, plain old high-quarter garden-variety sneakers are an excellent choice provided the terrain is not too rocky or rough. The flexible soles provide good traction; and because of their softness, sneakers enable the hunter to sense underfoot most twigs and branches before they snap. For readers who are Vietnam veterans, their GI jungle boots are excellent deer-hunting footwear provided the weather is not too cold and provided they will not be encountering much water. Even in a light snow, from two to three inches, these boots provide good traction and protection. There is no boot or shoe that I know of that gives better traction, especially on wet and slippery rocks, and these boots wear forever.

Shoe pacs are calf-length laceable boots with rubber lowers and leather uppers. These boots are good in almost any weather the hunter is likely to encounter except the very warmest or the most bitter cold. When properly conditioned with leather perservative, shoe pacs are waterproof for short-duration dunkings. All-leather boots of similar design to the shoe pacs are available, but these boots are harder to keep waterproofed. Neoprene or rubber-cork soles on either type of boot will give good traction.

Boots should be purchased one half-size larger than regular shoes to allow for extra socks. Be careful not to get the boot too big, or your foot will fit loosely. This will result in painful injury to the toes and toenails, especially when going down steep slopes in rugged terrain, since the toes will be jammed against the inside of the boot. While cotton socks are good enough for warm weather, light wool socks are a better choice. They will absorb moisture, help keep your feet dry, and extra pairs can be donned as the weather gets colder.

A good pair of gloves is a hunting necessity in cold climes. If the weather is not too cold, the knitted gloves available in any hardware store will do the job. Be sure to get them with leather palms and finger facings since the leather makes the rifle much easier to grasp. Leather gloves with woolen inserts are good hunting gloves, and an extra set of inserts can be carried in case they get wet. The main disadvantage of these gloves is that their bulkiness may slow you down trying to get your finger on the trigger. As popular as the knit and insert gloves are, I have never found a pair of either that kept my hands as warm as I would like on cold November stands in the late afternoon. My favorite gloves under such conditions are the shooters' mittens. Because of their mitten design as opposed to the individual finger design of gloves, the air does not circulate around each finger and the hand stays much warmer. An

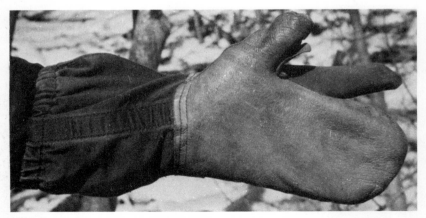

8–2 Mittens are much warmer than gloves, and the difference can be important in cold climates. Mittens for the hunter are available with trigger fingers. The mittens shown here have high elastic tops that pull over the coat sleeve to seal out the cold.

individual trigger finger is provided in these mittens for shooting. These gloves are slower than either of the others when it comes to getting off a shot, but when on stand, speed is usually not at a premium. A big advantage of most shooting mittens during snowy windy weather is that they have long uppers with elastic tops. The uppers are pulled up over the hunting coat, and the elastic completely seals the glove-coat gap and keeps snow from being blown up your arms and down into your gloves.

Hunting caps come in a variety of materials and designs depending on the use for which they are intended. Features to look for include a brim to keep the rain and snow from getting into your eyes and from running down your neck. Earflaps are essential in nippy weather. In very cold weather, the stocking cap worn by skiers and snowmobilers is good. If the face-covering part of the cap is not needed, it can be rolled up. But when the wind starts blowing and you are exercising every last ounce of control to avoid unnecessary movement on a stand or stalk, the face cover has great virtue. Get a cap that has one opening for eyes and nose. The larger opening makes it easier to use binoculars; the individual eye holes and nose holes have a way of shifting around till the eyeholes are up on your forehead and you're looking out through the nose hole with one eye. I find that any covering, whether it's a hood or a stocking cap, over my ears is annoying since I often hear deer before I see them. Hearing can be improved with either type of headgear by simply cutting holes in the sides large enough for sound passage but not so large as to expose the ears to the cold.

It may seem to the reader that all this discussion of clothing places undue emphasis on comfort. I don't think it's possible to place too much emphasis on comfort. I am convinced that improper clothing is one of the main reasons why deer hunters fidget on stand and give themselves away. It is next to impossible to remain motionless when you are colder than a well-digger's derriere, and I go to great extremes to make sure I'm comfortable while hunting. If the temperature is at all cold and I expect to be stand hunting, I carry a heavy fleece-lined parka rolled up on my back. This brown parka is too warm to wear while walking, so I wear my nice red coat as an outer garment until I get to my stand. Then I unroll and put on my snug warm parka, which was deliberately chosen in a size that fits easily over my hunting coat. About four o'clock in the afternoon, after I've been sitting on-stand for an hour, as the shadows are lengthening and a light snowy powder is being whipped through the air, that parka is worth its weight in winning lottery tickets. The boys in camp always get a few good laughs when they see me trudging off into the woods looking like a hunter's haberdashery. But they always seem to stop laughing when I have to come back in two trips: one trip to lug out my gear and another trip to retrieve the deer. For the last five years I have hunted heavily hunted public grounds. In that time I have bagged five deer with a total hunting time of twelve days, and that includes passing up some shots at spikehorns. I chalk up much of that success to knowing how to dress. Any nitwit can go into the woods on a cold day and be miserable — the trick is to be comfortable.

Binoculars

Binoculars are essential to the deer hunter regardless of the hunting technique that he employs. Binoculars trained on a section of apparently lifeless and sterile woods will disclose a flick of a tail here, a section of back there, and a raised head behind some bushes somewhere else. The contention that a rifle scope will serve just as well as a pair of binoculars is so much balderdash. A scope mounted on a rifle is awkward to use, has a limited field of view, does not give stereo viewing, and usually has much too low power.

Binoculars are described by a two-number rating, such as 6x30. The first number is the power of the binoculars. Thus a 6x30 pair of binoculars has a power of six and makes a deer 240 yards away look as if it were forty yards away. The second number is the diameter in millimeters of the objective (front) lens. The bigger this number is, the better the light-gathering ability of the binoculars and the heavier and bulkier they will be. Note that neither number tells you what the field of view is. It has become standard practice on better binoculars to stamp the field of view at 1,000 yards on the body of the binoculars. For example, the stamping 450' would mean a 450-foot field of view at 1,000 yards. Another way of designating the field of view is in degrees. One degree is equal to 52.5 feet at 1,000 yards. Therefore a pair of binoculars labeled 8° would have a field of view of 420 feet. Some binoculars have both labels. I use a set of 7x35 binoculars marked "Field 11°, 578 ft. at 1,000 yards." I have found 7x35 to be a good all-round size, although the 6x30, 7x50, and 8x35 are also popular. Any field of view from 7° to 12° will suffice, but I prefer the wider ones even though this makes for a bulkier glass. Select binoculars with coated lenses since the coating helps keep colors true to life, and this is important in spotting game. You can get a good pair of binoculars for from thirty to sixty dollars. If your eyes need individual corrections, be sure to get binoculars with individual adjustments on one or both barrels.

Binoculars help spot game in brushy country and allow the

hunter's vision to "penetrate" through the brush to some extent. If the binoculars are focused at seventy-five yards, for example, brush at fifty yards will be out of focus and less noticeable than objects at the focus distance. As a result, intervening twigs and branches seem to be partially removed from view since the eyes selectively settle on what is in focus. Binoculars are also a big help in picking up targets in the marginal light of early morning and late afternoon.

Even though most whitetail deer are shot at short ranges, it is amazing how many can be spotted at longer ranges if the hunter looks for the type of terrain and cover that will permit long-range spotting. Several years ago, I was hunting the mountain country of Orange County, New York. I had been on-stand for about an hour and a half with no luck and decided to stretch my legs and do a little stalking. It was mid-November, and the woods in this part of the state are gorgeous during the hunting season. The real peak of autumn foliage was just past, but the mountains were still cloaked with an ample supply of brilliant autumn leaves. They sky was a crisp, clear, autumnal blue with not a cloud in sight; and at an elevation of one or two thousand feet above the Hudson River, the scenery could not have been prettier.

I climbed up a high rocky hillside with a steep, bare, rocky face that one sees on many of the mountains in this area. The hill overlooked a small swampy valley on the other side of which there rose another peak of the ridge line along which I was hunting. This other peak, with was some six or seven hundred yards away, had a mountain field on top of it where the winds whistling over the ridge effectively kept any trees from taking hold. I decided to glass the field for late afternoon diners. Sure enough, there were half a dozen deer strolling around that field munching contentedly in the late afternoon sun. With the binoculars I was able to select a good route up the hill in view of the wind direction, which I could determine by observing the movement of the trees. The racks on the deer, if any, could not be seen at these ranges with my 7x35 binoculars, but there was no doubt that that hill needed relief from the weight of all that venison. It was too late in the afternoon to try to sneak up there that day, but I knew where to go the next day.

The following day I was on a stand overlooking the mountain field by three o'clock in the afternoon. I knew that the deer started to move about three thirty. They began to enter the field about three twenty-five, and I had a nice fat buck by three forty-five. The total hunting time that season was three hours the first day and forty-five minutes the second day, thanks to a good pair of binoculars.

Other Accessories

There are several other items that the hunter should carry with him. One is a high-quality knife. Both the folding and nonfolding types are adequate for the job, and selection between them is a matter of personal preference. If you get the folding type, be sure it has a strong positive blade-lock to lock the blade open, or you're liable to come out of your next carcass-dressing operation counting on your toes when you get past nine. With either knife, the extra money spent on a high-quality cutlery-steel blade will be money well spent. The better knives also have handles made of tough, impact-resistant materials. The handle should have a rippled or grooved surface. Smooth plastic handles become slick and hard to hold when wet with deer blood, which lubricates better than Quaker State 10w-30. The nonfolding hunting knives must have sheaths that are reinforced at the tip with metal. The metal-sheath tips, or a series of rivets around the tip of the sheath, keep the sharp knife point from penetrating the scabbard and into you should you fall on the knife. A knife that I find satisfactory is the Air Force's pilot-survival knife. These knives have a five-inch blade, hold an edge well, come with a honing stone in a pocket on the sheath, and have wrapped leather handles that stick to your hand like pine pitch even when wet. These knives cost from six to ten dollars.

Whatever kind of hunting knife you get, keep it sharp. The knife is meant to slice through what you want to cut, not forcefully tear it apart. Hunting pundits take great delight in describing for beginners the correct way to sharpen a knife on a stone. I find the whole technique unnecessarily laborious. The double-wheel knife sharpener designed for kitchen knives will do an excellent job on your game knife. Five or six passes through the sharpener and you are ready to go. Total sharpening time is five to ten seconds. Purists will no doubt raise more objections than a Philadelphia lawyer to this suggestion, but I have found that this method works quite well. It produces a knife that is sharp, cuts well, and has cutting edges close enough to the optimum angle so the edge holds well.

This next suggestion will also produce peals of laughter in some quarters, but I think it's a good idea to carry along a lightweight hatchet. Note that I am not talking here about the hunter-camper. The hunter who plans to camp out is obviously going to need a hatchet and a lot of other gear not discussed in this chapter. I am talking here about the one-day hunter who comes back in every day and sleeps at home. He will find that a hatchet comes in handy for many diverse jobs. I have never found a deer stand with which I was completely happy the way Mother Nature furnished it. I find that there are always branches, saplings, dead limbs, and the like that need to be trimmed. And each time I go back to the stand I spruce it up a little, trim a few more branches, and add a little more concealment. Sure, these jobs can be done with a knife, but only with the expenditure of about ten times as much effort. And when one is clearing away branches in a tree stand, the added length of the hatchet is handy because it extends the hunter's reach. When field-dressing a deer, I like to split the pelvis right in the woods. I find it gives me a cleaner, neater carcass. The job can be done with a knife if it weighs two pounds and has a three-foot handle on it. I use a lightweight (one-and-a-half-pound) stainless-steel hatchet that will take an edge that is sharper than a mother-in-law's tongue. Stainless steel has some tendency to chip, but if you don't chip it, it will hold its edge through several seasons with only minor touch-ups.

Don't venture out without a piece of rope from ten to fifteen feet long. Clothesline will do, but the nylon line used by boaters is less bulky for the same length and strength and does not rot as easily. If you have to pack your deer out, the rope can be used to tie his feet together so a pole can be slipped between them. If you hunt from trees, the rope can be tied around your bow or rifle to pull it up once you are up in the tree. If you pull your rifle up to you in this manner, please use this suggestion: tie the rope around the butt end of the stock or sling so the weapon won't be pointing at you as you pull it up! Also bring along an extra shoelace. It comes in handy if you break one and is useful when dressing out your deer (see Chapter 14).

If you are hunting in an area with which you are not very familiar, take along a map and a compass. If you are totally unfamiliar with the area, the map will give you some ideas about where to start hunting; you should you become misoriented (you should never let things get so out of hand as to become "lost"), the map will set you straight. Good maps for hunters are often available from state fish and game departments, and these maps are sometimes annotated with game notes. Excellent maps are also available from the U.S. Geological Survey. For maps east of the Mississippi, write to Branch of Distribution, U.S. Geological Survey, 1200 South Eads Street, Arlington, Virginia 22202. For maps west of the Mississippi, including Louisiana, write to Branch of Distribution, U.S. Geological Survey, Federal Center, Denver, Colorado 80225.

As a final note, when it comes to being comfortable, take along a snack. The following is the long-guarded secret family recipe for Donovan's World-Famous Whitetail Deer Hunter's Snack.

Dry roasted peanuts	Two handfuls
Raisins	Two handfuls
Chocolate chips	One handful

Mix thoroughly. Place in a stout plastic bag. If the weather is too warm, substitute M&Ms for the chocolate chips.

Part Three

The
Hunt

9

Woodsmanship

Every hunter who aspires to more than hit-or-miss success must become intimately familiar with the habits and spoor of his quarry. This knowledge comes only with prolonged exposure to and detailed study of the deer in his natural habitat. The purpose of this chapter is to familiarize the hunter with some of the more important features of deer tracks and deer signs and to point out some of the things that the hunter should look for in the field.

Tracks and Droppings

Deer tracks are very helpful to the hunter since they aid in detecting deer movements and in identifying likely crossings and runways. Conditions of soft earth or light snow must prevail if tracks are to be of greatest value, but even in normal dry fall conditions the observant hunter will detect enough tracks to be of great assistance to him. Soft spots near streams, along the margins of lakes, and in woodland depressions will all yield bits of information that can be pieced together by the hunter who knows how to interpret them.

The most obvious thing that one would like to be able to determine from deer tracks is the sex of the critter that poked the holes. It would be nice if does and illegal bucks had round hooves and legal bucks had square ones, so you could tell them apart. But they don't. So you can't.

It is true that there are certain generalizations that can be made about the tracks of big bucks, but with hunting pressure what it is today, most bucks don't get big. And the hot-stove-league stories that one hears about slenderness of hoof, spread of toes, roundness of toes, and other features that are supposed to distinguish between the sexes are so many pipe dreams. The feasibility of determining sex by hoofprint has actually been studied in detail by state fish and game departments, and no distinguishing characteristic has been found. I'm convinced that the only sure way that tracks can be used to determine sex is to follow the tracks until you find a deer standing in them. Such indicators as size, toe spread, and depth of impression are all fair indicators of size, but where I hunt, there are a lot more big does than big bucks.

Now that I've told you that sex can't be determined from tracks, I'm going to tell you how to do it. But realize at the outset that these indicators are uncertain indicators at best and apply only to big mature animals. So if you are a trophy hunter, here goes.

Attempts to sort out tracks by sex concentrate on two distinct aspects of the tracks. The first is the actual appearance of the track and any associated signs such as urine stains. The second is the line that the tracks take in going from one point to another. As far as the tracks themselves are concerned, the big buck seems to have a more careless and lackadaisical stride. His feet swing further out from the centerline of his line of travel and the toes have a slight tendency to toe out. In snow as shallow as three to four inches, a big buck will start to get lazy and won't bother to pick his feet up over the snow. Thus drag marks will be evident behind the print, and dewclaw impressions may be visible. Of course, as the snow get deeper, all deer leave drag marks.

While the mature buck may be more careless in his stride, when it comes to getting from one point to another he is far more businesslike. A doe will wander from side to side, back and forth, and will zigzag all over in the general direction of travel. In a moment of feminine frivolity, she will jump over a fallen log or scamper around a bit. If you are following a set of big tracks that behave in this manner, you are on the track of either a big doe or a buck with an identity crisis. In snow, urine stains are also helpful in determining sex. The buck will urinate in a hard stream that will penetrate the snow slightly ahead of his back feet in a fairly clean hole.

9–1   This track was left by a good-size buck that one of the author's hunting partners saw but at which he was unable to fire. Note the clear imprint of the dewclaws.

A doe, on the other hand, will spray a fairly large area when she urinates. Finally, when you have followed all these good buck-tracking tips and bump right into the back end of the fattest, sassiest female you've seen since you kissed your wife good-bye, don't say I didn't warn you. Nobody can really tell sex by tracks anyway.

It is also useful for the hunter to be able to tell the age of the tracks he finds. This is a difficult proposition. The best way to be sure that the tracks are fresh is to go out the day after a snowfall. Then you know that none of the tracks is more than one day old. And any time that you find a foot in one of the tracks, you can bet that the tracks are pretty fresh. Failing in both of these methods, check the definition of the tracks. In warm weather, snow tracks will soon start to melt and enlarge and lose their crisp definition. Don't be fooled into thinking that you are looking at the tracks of a large deer if it's just a case of melt-enlarged tracks. Tracks in soft

9-2 A small antlerless deer made this track. As the snow melts, the track will enlarge.
Don't be fooled!

earth also lose their form; but they do so more slowly, and in the
absence of rain such tracks may look fresh for several days to a
week. With a light breeze blowing, tracks in powdery snow will
look staler than last week's newspapers within minutes. In all of
these cases, it is useful to examine tracks that you know are fresh.
Check your own tracks, tracks of deer that you jump, and the tracks
of other hunters and wildlife. Look for such details as definition,
shininess of the bottom of the print (due to moisture), and the rate

9–3 A buck pawed up this piece of ground and urinated in it to stake out his territory and to attract does. The air was heavy with the smell of urine, the area was covered with fairly large tracks, and several saplings in the area had been rubbed recently.

at which tracks fill with snow or water. If you cross back over the tracks several hours later or at the end of the day, reexamine them for the effects of weathering. Check again the next day and several days later if you are still hunting the same area. It is only by such attention to detail that you will sharpen your tracking skills.

The average well-fed deer will decorate the countryside with ten to fifteen loads of droppings per day. Pellets are typically egg-shaped, about three-quarters of an inch long and half an inch in diameter. However, size and frequency of droppings vary with health and age of the animals and range conditions. The pellets resemble somewhat those of the porcupine and the snowshoe rabbit, but can be distinguished from them with a little practice. When first dropped, the pellets are shiny and black with a soft interior. With age, the pellets become duller and harder and eventually turn a dark brownish green before disintegrating into the soil.

Scrapes and Antler Rubs

Scrapes and antler rubs are familiar sights in deer country during the rut. Scrapes are circular areas on the ground from two to three feet in diameter where a buck has pawed away the leaves and an inch or two of the soil. The buck will urinate in the scrape during the rut and will visit the spot periodically to see if this clever device has lured any willing females into the area.

Antler rubs are found on springy young saplings that the restless buck uses for jousting partners. The rubs are the areas on the sapling where the bark has been worn away. The rubs are usually quite obvious since, if the rub is fresh, the newly exposed wood will be very light and the bark that has been worn away will usually be found in a shredded heap at the base of the tree. The area stripped of bark typically extends from halfway to three-quarters of the way around the tree, starts from six inches to a foot above the ground, and may go as high as three-and-a-half feet. Rubs will usually be found on, or close to, major runways and often three or four rubbed trees will be found within a few feet of one another. When you find a rub, peel a small strip of bark off the tree. By observing the color of the newly exposed bark and tree, you can get an estimate of the freshness of the rub.

Rubs and scrapes are lucrative hunting positions for the stand hunter. Since the buck's usual caution partially deserts him during the rut and since there is a good chance that he will come back several times a day to a given scrape or rub, the stand hunter who selects a well-concealed stand overlooking several fresh scrapes and rubs has a good chance of success.

9-4 Antler rubs. Here, the buck's enthusiasm resulted in a broken pine sapling.

9–5   More antler rubs. At left, a common woodland sight during the rut—two or more rubbed saplings in the immediate vicinity of one another. The bark shavings in the snow, above, attest to the fact that the rubbing activity occurred since the last snowfall.

ellaneous Observations

to the whitetail deer's bleat, which is rarely heard, the
s a snort that is heard all too often. To make the noise,
s his lungs full of air and then exhales through the nose
with a trumpeting whistle that can be heard two counties away.
The animal uses the snort as a warning device to warn other deer
in the area. The snort is often preceded by a stamping of
the forefoot on the ground in a slow drumming fashion. This
drumming is also meant to get the attention of other deer in the
area. Many a stalker has gotten his first indication of the presence
of deer when he was startled by this trumpeting warning signal,
which is usually followed by white flags disappearing over the hill.

I recall one occasion when I was sitting on a rocky out-
cropping on the side of a brushy hill using my binoculars to inspect
a likely draw below me. I was so engrossed that I didn't hear two
deer walk up to within fifteen yards of me. The first hint that I had
of their presence was two bellowing snorts that were so loud that I
thought sure I was about to be run over by a bull moose. Arms, binoculars, hat, and rifle all flew in different directions; and by the
time I regained my composure, I had slid halfway down the rock on
which I had been sitting. But I did manage to look up just in time
to see two deer depart through the bushes—and somehow it looked
like they were chuckling as they ran.

This incident illustrates another aspect of deer behavior that
sometimes works in the hunter's favor, but more often works
against him. Deer are curious to the point of being downright nosy.
Once in a while a stalk hunter will get his deer by looking behind
him and spotting a buck who just had to stick his head out to get a
better look at the hunter once he had passed. And now and then a
bow hunter will connect just because a curious deer felt compelled
to walk up to a hunter's tree for a detailed inspection of the big
ugly thing in the tree that smells so bad. But what happens more
often is this: the hunter will be sitting in his stand when some
puny antlerless animals walk out in front of him. With his adrenaline flowing and his heart beating a little faster, the hunter will
make some mistake. He will move his head too fast, move his rifle,
or in some other way alert one of the does. As soon as he does, the
hunter will freeze. But often it's too late. Once the doe sees something suspicious, her curiosity is aroused, and nothing short of an
earthquake or another hunter will keep her from satisfying it. She
will test the air. She will walk up closer. She will stop, sniff, paw,
and if necessary, come so close that her breath will fog up your binoculars (unless you are bow hunting and can shoot does, in which
case she'll stay just out of bow range). Then with a snort that alerts

every buck within a mile, she's gone; and you're left wishing that for just ten seconds the powers that be would declare an open season on nosy does.

When there are many other hunters moving about in the woods during the rut, bucks will be moving most of the day. However, in many hunting situations neither of these conditions prevails, and the hunter must rely on the natural movements of the deer. Deer commonly come down from their daytime beds to feed in the late afternoon and may even wait till dark if they are being heavily hunted. They will return before sunrise if pressed. Otherwise they will usually get back to their bedding areas an hour or two after sunrise. During the middle of the day, the stand hunter can normally expect a much reduced level of activity.

When moving along a runway, the older does lead the procession, followed by their fawns, and followed at a greater distance by any bucks that may be tagging along. The hunter who sets as his goal a deer of six points or more will have the mettle of his resolve sorely tested when he watches a procession of slick heads go by only to see a nice fat four-pointer follow the group two or three minutes later. To shoot or not to shoot, that is the question. There may be a bigger buck following along further back; then again, there may be nothing more than fragrant wisps of mountain air back there. And if there is a bigger buck following, he may spot the hunter and never show himself. And as every deer hunter knows, a deer on the meat pole is worth ten on the hill. But then again, that following buck may not be a six-pointer at all. He may be a record-book-size twelve-pointer. The true trophy hunter would have no doubt about what to do, but the average redcoat would probably find the temptation too great.

Knowing what deer do and don't like to eat will help the hunter locate likely feeding areas, and once the feeding areas are located he will be able to spot the runways leading to and from these areas. Deer are generally browsers as opposed to grazers and get most of their sustenance from the tender ends of secondary growth of hardwoods and conifers. High on their list of favorites in the north are such delicacies as oak, birch, maple, white cedar, and various evergreens. In the South, black titi, greenbriar, saw palmetto, and mushrooms account for a large portion of the diet. In the Southwest, black gum, acacia, white ash, and mesquite berries are favored fare. In all areas there is some grazing on various grasses, and water plants if available are usually highly sought after. Many types of nuts, such as acorns and beechnuts, are gourmet items, and an oak grove with no evidence of acorns on the ground during the fall is a sure indicator of deer activity. Squirrels, of course, also like the acorns, but they will leave gnawed-up shells lying around as evidence of their activity. Deer, on the other hand, come through like so many vacuum cleaners and ingest anything not affixed to the ground with roots.

Deer-browsed vegetation is easily recognized. The tender ends of the plant are chewed off with a rough jagged edge. The browsing is usually done at about waist height, but anything from ground level to about fifty-six inches above the ground may be hit. Anything above fifty-six inches might as well be growing in the forest canopy since few deer can reach higher than this even standing on their back legs.

In agricultural areas, deer show considerable affinity for almost anything the farmer grows. When my family lived in Vermont, deer seemed to take an inordinate amount of interest in our corn and lettuce patches. We once made the mistake of going on a trip for several days and taking our dog with us. Upon returning home, as we drove back up the hill to the house in our old 1932 Chevy (which made more noise than a cement mixer full of large rocks), white tails could be seen lighting out of the garden in all directions. They really weren't going too fast. In fact, they kind of lumbered with an occasional stop for a burp. There wasn't enough left of my family's garden to make a tossed salad for a midget on a diet.

Deer are not above munching on rye and wheat and will go out of their way for some fresh corn. They seem especially to like the corn when it is just sprouting up out of the ground, and at this time of year the poor farmer must be on guard against crows in the daytime and deer at night.

Developing Woodsmanship

A first-rate hunter is knowledgeable in the ways of the woods and takes pride in his knowledge and ability. He knows how to camp and backpack. He is a marksman who knows his weapon and knows what he can and cannot hit. And above all, he knows the ways of the game that he hunts. He can read and interpret signs where the novice sees nothing.

This degree of expertise comes only with long and patient practice and many hours spent in the woods. Preseason scouting trips not only help locate promising hunting areas, but also give the hunter practice in reading signs and stalking game. After reading the chapter on marksmanship, the reader will probably think that I am notebook happy if I suggest he keep another notebook. But there is one more area in which I think that such notes can be invaluable. I have a notebook in which I keep tabs of the conditions under which I shoot each deer. I make a simple sketch of the area and note such factors as wind conditions, ranges, animal size, ammunition used, and the like. In thumbing back through the book, it is educational to note the circumstances under which each successful hunt was made. Certain techniques seem to prove successful over and over again. Each hunt provides its own lessons, and the serious hunter can learn a lot from these lessons.

The results of preseason scouting trips can also be noted in such a notebook, making it easier to locate chosen crossings and tentatively selected stands or drive areas. The true naturalist-hunter will also take pleasure in noting facts about tracks, rubs, animal behavior, and other related facts. The following pages are reproduced from my notebook and record the results of a recent successful hunt in Virginia.

9–6

WHITETAIL DEER

1. DATE   22 Nov 74

2. TIME   0805

3. PLACE   GOODE'S MTN, VA.

4. WEATHER   CLEAR, CRISP ~25°
               VERY LIGHT BREEZE, ~5" OF SNOW
               FELL DURING PREVIOUS NIGHT

5. BUCK, 7 POINTS
   DRESSED WEIGHT   155 #, 110# FREEZER
        WRAPPED
   GUN   03 SPRINGFIELD
   AMMO   FEDERAL, 180 GRAIN
   SHOTS   1

6.   THE PREVIOUS DAY I HAD STALKED THOUGH
       THIS AREA AND FOUND WELL WORN &
       APPARENTLY HEAVILY TRAVELLED RUNWAYS
       THROUGH THE SADDLE BETWEEN TWO
       RISES ON THE NORTH END OF GOODE'S
       MTN. I ALSO FOUND SOME RECENTLY
       RUBBED TREES AND A SCRAPE THAT
       LOOKED A LITTLE STALE. THERE WERE
       SEVERAL SETS OF FAIRLY LARGE TRACKS
       IN THE AREA. I DECIDED TO TAKE A
       STAND THERE THE NEXT MORNING &
       FOUND A BLOWN DOWN TREE THAT
       WAS EASY TO CLIMB & GAVE A GOOD
       VIEW OF THE AREA. THE NEXT

MORNING I WAS UP IN THE BLOWN DOWN
TREE JUST AS THE SUN WAS BREAKING
OVER THE RIDGE. ABOUT 0750 I HEARD
MOVEMENT TO THE SOUTHWEST. I COULD
SEE IT WAS A BUCK, BUT WAS UNABLE
TO GET A CLEAR SHOT FOR ABOUT 15
MINUTES. HE MOVED INTO THE OPENING
OF THE SADDLE, PAUSED, AND I DROPPED
HIM WITH ONE SHOT.

7.

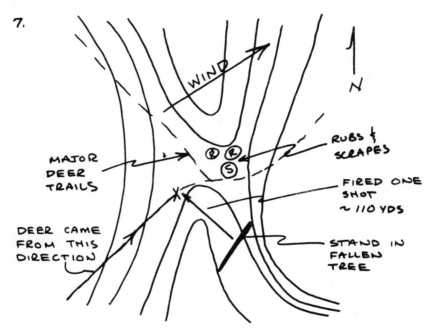

9–7

10

Standing

Bagging a whitetail buck is surprisingly difficult in most parts of the country. It is particularly difficult in the heavily hunted Northeastern and Central Atlantic states. In a recent year in Virginia, one deer hunter in eight was successful. In New York it was one in twelve; and in Vermont, one in ten. This means that in this part of the country something like nine out of ten deer hunters return from the field every year empty-handed. If I had to recommend a simple technique that properly executed would improve significantly the average deer hunter's chances of beating these odds, that technique would be standing.

10-1 This sequence of photos shows the advantage that the hunter gets by selecting an elevated stand and by separating himself from the area where he expects deer to appear. The first photo shows the view of an open field that the hunter gets from a stand high in some rocks. The second photo, looking back at the hunter from the field from about 50 yards, shows that the hunter is hardly visible. In the third photo, from about 150 yards, the hunter is so distant and elevated that even a great deal of hunter movement would probably go unnoticed by deer. The author killed two deer from this stand in Orange County, New York, in two successive seasons with about three hours of total hunting time.

Standing Techniques

Standing consists of selecting a spot where you think a deer will pass and then stationing yourself where you can observe the spot until one does so. It sounds very simple, but it isn't.

The selection of a stand is a two-part process. First the section of feeding ground or runway to be observed must be selected, and then the location of the stand with respect to that runway or feeding ground must be chosen.

The telltale signs of active runways and feeding areas were described in the previous chapter. The stand hunter will usually do well to station himself on a runway between feeding area and bedding area before sunrise to catch deer returning to their beds, or late in the afternoon to catch them coming down to feed. Typically, the beds are on hillsides, in high saddles, and on, or near, ridges. The feeding areas are often at lower elevations along lakes, in fields, and in grandma's garden patch. Hence hunter's often speak of deer "coming down" in the afternoon and "going back up" in the early morning. If the deer make it all the way down to the feeding area before sunset, the feeding area itself may provide a good place for a stand. If they move too slowly to get to the feeding areas before dark, stands will have to be selected on the runways between beds and feeding areas in order to insure adequate daylight for shooting. During the rut, the rubs and scrapes described in Chapter 9 also provide good locations for stands.

Most redcoats do a fair job of choosing an area likely to be traversed by deer, but they foul up the rest of the selection process. The stand, naturally, must be chosen downwind of the target area and downwind of any path that the deer are likely to follow to get to the target area. (The target area is the area in which you expect the deer to be when you shoot.) But most hunters make the mistake of choosing a stand that is much too close to where they expect the deer to appear. It is true that in some areas the brush and secondary growth are so heavy that long shots are impossible. But in most semiopen timber areas and broken farmland, the hunter should, with some judicious scouting, be able to find a stand between 150 and 200 yards from where he expects the deer to present itself for a shot. With modern high-powered rifles and proper sights, lethal shots on standing or slowly moving targets at these ranges should be no problem. The reason for getting all this distance between you and the deer is to keep the deer from spotting or smelling you before you spot him. Most hunters on stands suffer from a terrible malady that I call the "itchy fidgets." They squirm and move and wiggle and wonder why they never see any deer. You can get away with a lot more squirming and wiggling at 200 yards than you can at fifty yards.

Stand in orchard (low)

Deer's trail from bedding area to orchard

Alternate stand on hill (high)

10–2 In many areas, deer come down from bedding areas to feeding areas at lower elevations in the late afternoon. If their movement habits are such that they get to the feeding areas while it's still light enough for shooting, the hunter can take a low stand in a feeding area such as the orchard shown in this illustration. If, however, the deer don't get to their feeding areas until after dark, a stand in the feeding area will do no good. In such a situation a stand higher up on the hillside might enable the hunter to intercept deer en route from their beds to their feeding areas while there is still enough light left for shooting.

144

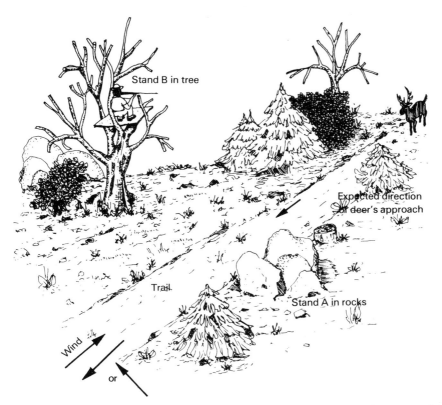

10-3 If the hunter has selected a section of trail which he wants to hunt from a stand, it is usually a good idea to pick two stands from which the trail in question can be observed. The wind direction may make one of the stands unusable.

Another way to make minor movements less detectable by deer is to select an elevated stand in a tree or on a steep hillside. Before you go climbing up a tree, check your local game laws since elevated stands are illegal in a few areas. They are, however, legal in most areas, and where legal they are extremely effective. Deer just don't seem to look up for danger. They expect it to come at them along the ground, and of course, it usually does. The hunter in a tree stand 200 yards away from a deer can do a jig in the tree and go undetected, whereas the same motion on the ground would send white flags flying in all directions. The elevated stand also serves to keep the hunter's scent off the ground and thus makes those annoying shifts in wind direction less important. Just how well-concealed the tree stander can be was brought home to me one day while I was bow hunting in a pine stand on the edge of a field. I had chosen a stand about eight feet up in a pine tree and had carefully cleared out openings through the branches in the directions that I thought were most likely for shots. But I had failed to take Murphy's Law into account. Murphy's Law for deer hunters states, "No matter how carefully you check the trails around your stand, no matter how much effort you put into deciding in advance the deer's direction of approach, nine times out of ten the deer will come up on you from a totally unanticipated direction." And that's just what a rambunctious little spikehorn did to me that day. He came ambling through the brush without a care in the world and walked right under my tree along a route that didn't leave me a prayer for a shot. And since white pine trees grow thick branches close together, I could not even shoot straight down. Who would have thought to clear out branches for a straight-down shot from a height of eight feet? Certainly not me. So there I sat with this buck standing right underneath me, so close that when he raised his head his antlers couldn't have been more than four or five feet from the soles of my boots. At a distance of five feet, it doesn't take a particularly alert deer to smell a hunter. (I've known hunters that even I could smell at five feet.) Or maybe I had my shirt unbuttoned and he heard my heart beating. In any event, something prompted that buck to tip his head back and look straight up. Those two big eyes of his opened up to the size of saucepans. He wasn't sure what it was that was sitting up in that tree, but it was too big for a chipmunk and too ugly for a bear. He gave a quick snort, did a hairpin turn, and took three big jumps down the safe brushy path he had just come up. He continued on down the path walking slowly, stepping high, and pausing every few steps for another look back at that suspicious pine tree.

Several object lessons can be learned from this experience. For one thing, it illustrates just how vulnerable deer are to danger from above. If I had a ten-pound rock instead of that bow, I might have gotten that buck. If the openings through the branches had been a little bigger, I could have jumped on him and ridden him to the check-in station. Deer just don't look up.

Also note that I said I heard this deer before I saw him. Of all the deer that I have spotted from stands at ranges of less than 100 yards, four out of five I heard before I saw. Deer are not particularly cautious or quiet when moving through the woods if their suspicions have not been aroused, and the stand hunter soon learns to distinguish between deer noises and the rustling antics of squirrels and birds.

Having spent many cold windy hours precariously perched in a tree waiting for my Boone and Crockett trophy to come strolling down the path, I have had much time to reflect on such subtleties as the desirability of one species of tree compared to another

10–4 If the wind isn't blowing too hard, a hunter on-stand can usually hear a deer walking through the snow at some distance. This unalerted forkhorn will make a fairly rhythmic "crunch, crunch, crunch" noise as he travels. (Courtesy of Virginia Commission of Game and Inland Fisheries)

for standing. My favorite is the white pine. These trees are usually easy to climb since they have circles of branches radiating out from the trunk at one-foot to two-foot intervals, and the branches usually start close enough to the ground to be easily reached. (I find it very difficult to shinny up the lower ten or fifteen feet of a tree trunk to reach the first branch in full hunting regalia.) Once up in the tree, the branching pattern of white pines is such that it is usually easy to find a comfortable position and still have one's legs resting on a lower branch. Nothing will cause you to be uncomfortable faster than to have your legs dangling in an unsupported fashion while sitting on a branch. Another big advantage of the pine is that it keeps its thick green foliage all year round. This provides the hunter with a ready-made blind that will help mask some of his movements. This same thickness may also necessitate the clearing of a few "windows" through the branches for shooting purposes, but this is a simple matter and can usually be done with a few quick swings of a hatchet. It is not enough just to clear out a window to see through. Actually get into firing position and make sure that there are no obstructing branches or twigs that will interfere with your shot in any of the directions in which you expect to fire. This precaution is especially important in the case of the bow hunter. Your position in the tree may be very comfortable, but as

10–5 In a pine-tree stand, note how quickly the hunter becomes "invisible." The photos were taken from five, twenty-five, and seventy-five yards. Note also how much better the hunter is concealed in the evergreen pine tree than he would be if he were in one of the nearby leafless trees.

you rise and draw your bow you may well find several branches in your way if you don't take care to clear them out in advance.

Comfort in the stand is of paramount importance because it is the hunter's comfort or lack thereof that is the primary determinant of how long his patience will hold out and how long he can remain motionless. Unfortunately, the average human derriere is not comfortable pressed against a cold, hard, tree limb. If it were comfortable, we could just furnish our homes with logs, stumps, and branches in lieu of easy chairs and sofas. But there are ways to make that inhospitable branch more inviting. A rolled up piece of bulky cloth or beach towel will take much of the sting out of that limb. Better yet, a padded or inflatable cushion, such as the ones football fans take to the stadium with them, are inexpensive, are easy to carry, and are great bottom fatigue reducers.

I prefer portable devices, such as pillows and cushions, to permanent structures for stands, because I often shift stands during a season and do not greatly relish carrying lumber, hammer, saws, and so forth in to the woods to build elaborate stands. But for those who know just where they want to hunt and who don't plan to move much, a permanent stand built before the season might be just the thing. The degree of elaborateness can be varied to suit your tastes, and the stand can be anything from a simple open platform to an enclosed structure with all the creature comforts.

Ground-level blinds do a good job of offsetting some of the hunter's disadvantage if he is forced to stand-hunt at ground level. Ground-level blinds can usually be built out of materials available in the woods; and if the cover on the blind is made thick enough, it will help protect the hunter from the elements as well as from visual detection by the deer. A blind or stand of any type, on the ground or elevated, should be built a minimum of several months before the season starts to allow the deer to become accustomed to it. If you just climb a tree and lop off a few branches, deer will get over this disturbance in less than an hour. If you are planning a major preseason construction effort, the early spring is a good time to go since the woods at this time of year retain much of the appearance that they have in the fall and the visibility conditions are similar to the fall because of the sparseness of the foliage.

In fifteen years of military service, I hunted on more military posts than most folks even know exist, and I learned about a very interesting way to stand-hunt one day on a base. In the fall of 1969, I was hunting at the Quantico Marine Corps Base in eastern Virginia. I was walking across a field and was exercising little caution since I was heading for a preselected stand; suddenly I jumped several deer out of a long, shallow depression in the field. After recovering from my initial chagrin at seeing all those white tails bounding off into a distant tree line, I decided to go down into the depression and look it over. The draw was damp, the grass and plants in it were still green as opposed to dry and brown like the rest of the field, and there were many signs of deer activity throughout the area. It occurred to me that this might be an excellent place to stand-hunt, but a slight problem came to light. There wasn't a tree, stump, rock, or bush within 300 yards that offered visibility down the draw. I decided at once against taking a stand in the middle of the field and hoping to remain motionless long enough to fool a deer. My friends all tell me that I do a terrible imitation of an apple tree. But a little bit of scouting around the field provided a solution. It seems that the leathernecks used this field for maneuvers; and in addition to the usual post-maneuver debris, such as old C-ration cans and extended cartridge cases, there were foxholes. That's right, foxholes. And these were no ordinary, open, unimproved foxholes. These were all covered and neatly camouflaged and in the finest tradition of the Marines defending a hill; these foxholes afforded excellent visibility and fields of fire. So I just climbed right into one and settled down for a long wait. But it turned out that I didn't have very long to wait. Within fifteen minutes, the first doe returned to finish her interrupted dinner; and by the time I crawled out of that foxhole at dusk, I had watched six antlerless deer and one spikehorn feed in that draw. I didn't shoot the spike because I was after something a little bigger that day, but I sure learned a new way to stand-hunt for deer.

Foxhole stands have several important advantages. For one, they are a lot warmer than an above-ground blind on a bitter-cold, windy day. Foxholes can even be heated with catalytic heaters if necessary. A ledge dug into the side of the foxhole can be outfitted with a cushion for comfort, and stretching and wiggling your legs is all done below ground level. In certain types of vegetation, such as dense young pines, visibility is actually better at ground level because the hunter is looking under low-lying boughs.

The depth of the hole will depend on several factors, not the least of which is your stamina at digging. The deeper the hole, the more work involved, but less of your body is exposed to view and to the elements. In some types of terrain you cannot dig down to shoulder depth because your eyes must be a foot or more above ground level to insure adequate visibility. In some cases a shallow foxhole can be combined with an above-ground blind if the blind affords some protection and screening for that part of the hunter's body that remains above the top of the foxhole.

Foxholes should be covered to keep heat in and snow and

rain out. Pine branches serve this purpose admirably. A thermos of hot coffee and a bag full of Donovan's World-Famous Whitetail Deer Hunter's Snack (see Chapter 8), and you'll be so comfortable that you'll run the risk of falling asleep on your stand.

Advantages of Standing

I am a solo hunter. I have nothing against drives and related techniques in which several hunters combine forces, but I find that much of the satisfaction in hunting comes from pitting myself against the animal. I don't even like to stand-hunt in areas where there are other hunters kicking up the deer for me. I prefer to pack in to the less hunted areas where it is possible to go for days without seeing another hunter. I spend altogether too much of my life behind a desk, talking to people, fighting traffic, and otherwise being folded, stapled, spindled, and mutilated. Deer season is an opportunity to get away from all this and to get back into the type of untouched forest and pristine wilderness that most people never get to see firsthand.

The really patient stander gets to see the woods in a state that eludes all but the most ardent naturalist. For hours at a time the stand hunter will be privileged to observe the ebb and flow of natural woodland activity in as nearly undisturbed a state as possible. Consider, for example, birds. They provide no end of entertainment for the stand hunter. While in a tree stand I have had chickadees land on my bow and attempt to pull off my cloth bowstring silencers. I have had a blue jay attempt petty larceny on my lens cap covers. While on stands either hunting or photographing I have watched ospreys and bald eagles, blue herons and pileated woodpeckers. Cardinals flit about in the autumn woods in Virginia with a plumage that puts the redcoats to shame when it comes to brilliance and beauty.

The animals are no less pleasant to observe. Foremost are the deer themselves. So much can be learned about these beautiful creatures by just watching them, and only the stand hunter gets to watch them for hours at a time. What and how the deer eat can be observed at length. The stand hunter can test the deer's senses with slight movements and low-level noises to see what alarms them, and at the end of the day he can try stalking to see how close he can get before the deer take flight.

Raccoons will amble past the stand hunter's position following an erratic, zigzag path that is understood only by God and raccoons. I once had one of these intriguing little fellows actually start up the tree I was in, realize that something was wrong although he

10-6 Tree stands preferably prepared in advance of the season, are easy to build, afford good visibility, make the hunter's position more comfortable, and make shooting easier.

10–7 This stand in the rocks took little effort to prepare, yet from the deer's point of view the hunter is nearly invisible.

wasn't sure just what, turn around, and head elsewhere. Gray squirrels will run right over you if you're not careful and clean the peanuts out of your pockets as they pass.

The majesty of the fall and winter woods is itself something that can be fully appreciated only with the prolonged exposure that a stander gets. At times the silence is awesome. At other times the cacaphony is unbelievable. And always the scenic grandeur is nothing less than humbling.

There is one last advantage I would like to catalog for stand hunting: it is highly effective. Whatever spiritual rejuvenation may attach to sitting for hours in the woods, I know of nothing more aesthetically satisfying than a good hot bowl of venison stew served up in front of the fireplace on a cold January night. And stand hunting will provide the venison for that stew more assuredly than any other hunting method I know.

10–8 Foxholes can provide a means of concealment in otherwise open terrain. They also provide considerable protection from cold, windy weather. Prepare foxholes well in advance of the hunting season and be sure that they are legal in your area. Also be sure that you have the landowner's permission.

11

Stalking and Floating

Stalking, or still hunting as it is often called, is the ultimate expression of the hunter's art. Simply stated, stalking is the art of moving quietly and slowly through the
woods until you literally sneak up to within shooting
range of a deer. This type of hunting is sometimes referred to as "still hunting"; the word "still" is used in
the sense of silent or quiet. However, many people hear
the term and confuse this method with the method of
standing that was described in the previous chapter.
Since the term "stalking" eliminates this confusion and
is also a better description of the method, it will be
used throughout this book.

Stalking Technique

Stalking is the ultimate form of whitetail deer hunting
because it pits hunter against deer on the deer's terms.
It is a game of stealth and wits for which the deer is better equipped. Sneaking up on a whitetail buck is no
easy feat, and the hunter who successfully brings down
his deer by this method can take justifiable pride in his

:omplishment. In addition to the sense of accomplishment that it affords the hunter, stalking has another big advantage: it produces a lot of picnic-basket-size racks for those skilled in the art. Big old bucks tend to get cagey during the hunting season; and while the stander may pick off a lot of spikes and forkhorns, it is the skillful stalker who has the best chance of perforating a smart old hide with a large rack growing out of one end. In addition, standing is not productive during the middle of the day in many areas. Stalking provides a profitable use for the hours of midday and lets the hunter who has been on-stand all morning walk some of the stiffness out of his joints.

If one factor had to be singled out for the average hunter's lack of success when he attempts to stalk, that factor would have to be impatience. Stalking is not the same as hiking or walking. The walker comes in after a day of hunting and says something like, "I saw eighteen white tails today, but I didn't get a shot." If someone says this to you, you have just seen a dumb hunter. Stalking must be done very slowly, covering little ground, and employing great concentration. It is a very tiring way to hunt if properly done. A good stalker travels between four hundred and one thousand yards in an hour. To get an idea of how slow this is, go out into the woods and walk about as slowly as you can possibly discipline yourself to go. Then, when you stalk, travel about half that speed. You'll only be going a little bit too fast.

The stalker's most effective weapons are his eyes. He must consistently spot deer before they spot him if he is to be consistently successful. Take a step and stop and look. Look twice. Look for a flick of a tail, an ear, a raised head, or the horizontal line of the back. With the exception of those deer detected by movement and noise, I have probably spotted more deer by picking up the curved line of the rump than I have by any other feature. The legs look like so many saplings. The head, ears, and antlers resemble branches, crooked tree trunks, and clumps of leaves. In some areas there are many fallen trees that provide the woods with long horizontal lines that look like a deer's back. But the large smooth curve of the rump is not typical of the woodland scene, and the eye is quick to pick it up.

Some stalkers like to use binoculars. In certain types of open terrain with extended visibility, binoculars can be useful. They will enable the hunter to pick up forms long before he would have seen them with the naked eye. But under most stalking conditions, where the hunter is focusing his eyes first at ten yards, and then at a hundred yards, binoculars are more trouble than they are worth. A stalker should maker every effort to move his arms and upper body as little as possible, and the constant lifting and lowering of binoculars defeats this purpose. The stalker must move through the woods like a cat at worst and like a puff of smoke at best.

One disadvantage of stalking is that the shots afforded to the stalker are not nearly as good as those the stander gets. The stalker with high standards of sportsmanship must pass up many marginal shots, even if he is a fair-to-middling snapshooter; and if he is not a good snapshooter, he must pass up even more shots. This is not meant to imply that the stalker only gets to shoot at running game. The practiced stalker will sneak right up on some deer and will get excellent shots at standing game. Of course, most of these shots will, of necessity, be taken from the offhand position. The stalker will often get good standing shots at deer even after he jumps them. Why? Because the stalker is moving with such stealth that most of the deer he spooks won't be panicked into headlong flight. Often they will only go ten or twenty yards before they stop for a little better look at what it was that frightened them. The wise stalker raises his gun when he sees the flags; so he is all ready and in position when that big buck stops to satisfy his curiosity with one last fatal look.

Stalking can be done by two or more hunters working together; and in this instance the technique takes on some of the characteristics of driving, but it is still stalking and not driving. This type of stalking is done most commonly by two men working abreast, or in line, with no standers posted as would be done in a drive. In this type of hunting, safety is a paramount concern and the stalker must be positive exactly where his partner is at all times or else he absolutely must not shoot. The problem of keeping track of your partner is much harder when hunting abreast than when hunting in line. The best way I have found to maintain contact with a partner is through the sparing use of game calls. If you and your partner each have a crow call, for example, an occasional "caw" blown on the call should keep each of you pretty well informed of the other's position.

The object of stalking with a partner instead of alone is to try to intercept some of the deer that would circle around or slip by the solo hunter. Once a deer is spooked, he fixes all of his attention on the hunter that frightened him. The deer will try to circle around the hunter or slip by him while staying out of sight. The deer will sometimes become so engrossed in evading the first hunter that he will darn near walk right over the second. Two men hunting abreast will do well to have one stalk along a ridge line and the other stalk fifty to 100 yards down the side of the ridge. Deer jumped on a ridge will not usually run along the ridge. They will run downhill; and if they run down the right side, your partner may get a shot. Similarly, deer spooked from below will head up

First stalker

Trail

Deer circles back off trail

Second stalker gets the shot

Second stalker

11–1 The two-man stalk can be very effective. Hunters can stalk either in line (tandem) or abreast, but in either case they must keep each other in visual contact for safety's sake. When tandem stalking, it is often the second hunter who gets the shot as the deer tries to circle around.

for the ridge and may cross over it. This may give the man at the top a shot. Another good method is to hunt brush clumps and thick patches of growth like rhododendron with one hunter penetrating the growth and the other circling around it.

When it is suggested that two stalkers hunt in line (one behind the other), the trail man (the one behind) often feels that he is getting the short end of the deal. He instinctively feels that the lead man will get most of the shots. This is not the case. As far as I can determine, the trail man gets as many or more shots. The lead man spooks nearly all of the deer. Many of these deer slip away unnoticed by the lead man, and because of their propensity to rivet all their attention on the lead hunter as they circle, the trail man gets more than his share of shots. From fifty to 100 yards is a good interval for this type of hunt. The trail man should keep the lead hunter in visual contact at all times for reasons of safety.

When and Where to Stalk

Stalking is much more difficult under some ground and weather conditions than others. No one can move silently through a ground covering of leaves that are as crisp as cornflakes. But the thing to remember is that no other creatures move silently through such leaves, and the deer expect to hear some noises. Thus the trick is to make your leaf-rustling sound like the natural woodland sounds of birds and squirrels. This means that you must avoid the rythmic "crunch, crunch, crunch" of steady walking and the "thump, thump, thump" of heavy footfalls that make you sound like an infantry platoon. Take a rustling step or two, being as quiet as possible, and then stop and wait. And look. And listen. Remember that unalerted deer make just about as much noise moving through the woods as you do, and if you are making a special effort to be quiet, they may actually be making more noise than you.

A good drenching rain before the stalk is a boon to the hunter. The rain dampens the leaves into near silence, and the dampness makes telltale twigs more likely to bend than to snap. And deer like to get up, stretch their legs, and move about in search of food after having been confined by a driving rain. I don't even mind a light misty rain during the stalk itself, and during a light rain is a good time to sneak up on deer holed up for the duration of the foul weather. Hunting in a heavy rain is no great fun; but if you are on a limited vacation for hunting and the weather you ordered doesn't show up, you may have no choice. Wear a rubberized rain suit, pants, a hooded jacket, and a wool shirt and wool pants over the rain suit. The wool will become drenched but will retain its good insulating and silencing properties, and you will stay fairly dry.

One condition that makes it almost impossible to stalk is crusted snow. The deer will hear your big size twelves coming a mile away, and you'll be lucky even to see very many tails. There is only one type of stalking that I know of that pays off well under such circumstances. Since I developed the technique on my own (although I'm sure many others have used it), I'll take the liberty of

Wind—
any of
these directions

11-2 Cresting consists of stalking as quietly as possible to a ridgeline or hilltop and then easing into a position where a large expanse of the hilltop or the far side of the ridge becomes visible. This method is useful for any ground and weather conditions, but may be the only effective stalking technique when the walking is very noisy as is the case with crusted snow.

giving it a name: cresting. Cresting consists of walking deliberately but without undue noise up the side of a hill or mountain toward the ridge and doing it in such a manner that you are heading into the wind. When you get within from thirty to fifty yards of the ridge line, start stalking as best you can even if the snow crunches. The critical time comes when you approach the ridge itself. There will usually come a point where you take one or two steps and a major portion of the top of the ridge becomes visible. Freeze and scan. It is here that you may spot deer. Until you crested over the ridge line, you were hidden from the deer's view. Much of the noise you made was hidden from them because of the intervening hillside. In addition, the wind was blowing toward you and tended to carry any noises away from the deer. The wind also helped by carrying your scent away. A pair of binoculars is a great assistance in this type of hunting.

If you don't spot any deer along the ridge, continue as quietly as possible across the ridge, and crest over the far side. Just as when you went up the hill, there will be a point where suddenly you can see a large expanse of hill on the far side that had been screened from your view. Freeze and carefully investigate this new area inch by inch with your binoculars. Once you have carefully probed the entire area with your binoculars, go and check it all again. Many a time I have checked a section of woods like this with binoculars until I was sure nothing was there, only to see white tails scattering in all directions as I proceeded to walk into the area. If you convince yourself there are no deer on the far side either, walk back over the crest to the downwind side of the hill where you started, walk along the side of the hill parallel to the ridge for several hundred yards, then crest the ridge again.

Cresting is a useful technique whether the ground is noisy or not. I have used it during the bow season to pop up on deer feeding along the ridges at ranges of less than thirty yards.

Old logging roads are a good choice for stalking because the hunter can usually move more silently along the road because of the lack of undergrowth. For similar reasons game trails are good. Ridge lines with rocky outcroppings and heavy moss cover also provide the hunter with unusually quiet footing. Pine needles are another quiet ground covering for stalking.

A good stiff breeze will make enough natural noise to cover up most of the noise the hunter makes, and for this reason some hunters prefer to stalk on windy days. However, my experience has been that on windy days the deer seem more nervous than a trophy moose at a Boone and Crockett banquet. The deer seem to sense that the protective value of their sense of hearing has been largely

fied and this makes them uneasy. And, of course, the hunter
loses the usefulness of his sense of hearing. Since many of the
deer a stalker spots are first detected by hearing them, this is a serious handicap.

I recall a backpack hunting trip several years ago into the
mountains of western Viginia where the wind really worked in my
favor on a stalk. My alarm clock failed to go off in the tent on the
first morning of the hunt (because I had rolled over on it in my
sleep), and I woke up about half an hour later than I had planned. I
woke up my partner, rushed around the inside of the tent getting
dressed, unzipped the tent flap, and stepped outside only to find
that we had been visited with four to six inches of snow during the
night. Hurriedly I loaded up my .30/06, pulled on my hunting
gloves, and struck out for the stand I had selected the previous day.
The stand was about half a mile away, the terrain was rough, and
as I pushed along to get to my stand before the sun came over the
ridge line, I managed to work up a good sweat. As a result, when I
finally got to my stand, which was at ground level near the base of
a tree, I was pretty damp and overheated. I plopped down, somewhat relieved that it hadn't gotten too light before I got into position, and prepared to rest up a little.

One thing I hadn't noticed until I sat down, though, was that
in addition to snowing it had gotten considerably colder during the
night. And then a good stiff wind came up and whipped along the
ridge line kicking up little swirls of the powdery snow and periodically dumping them all over me. What with my damp and overheated condition, the cold temperature, and the snowy gusts of
wind, it was only from forty five minutes to an hour before I had
taken about all that I could take. I was thoroughly frozen.

I stood up, shook off the snow, and glassed the area with binoculars. Nothing. I decided to try stalking down the ridge into the
wind and away from camp. The snow was powdery, but still managed to crunch quite loudly with each step. Yet the wind was blowing toward me and was pretty strong; so I hoped to be able to get
away with all the noise I was making.

The woods in this area consisted of a mature open stand of
oaks interspersed with occasional Virginia pines, so the visibility
was pretty good. I had not been stalking long, in fact only about fifteen minutes, when I thought I could hear a fairly steady "crunch,
crunch, crunch" in the snow, but the wind made it difficult to tell
the direction from which it was coming. Twice I stopped, listened,
and searched, but was unable to locate the source of the noise. Still
the noise persisted. I stopped a third time. This time I saw some-

thing that almost made my heart stop. About forty yards to my right front a large buck stepped out from between several large oaks that had been blocking my view. I didn't have time to count points, but I knew that that rack was a big one.

The buck still hadn't spotted me. This was partly because of the strong wind that was blowing from him to me, partly because of my very slow movements, and partly, I expect, because of dumb luck. I am not one, however, to question a little stroke of luck—at least not good luck. I slipped the safety off my rifle, picked that deer up in my scope, cursed myself for having left the variable scope on four power, which was much too much magnification for this short range, and fired one shot into what I judged to be that old buck's boiler room.

That deer lit out like he hadn't been touched. He ran straight toward me, spotted me, turned, and bolted down the hill in a flash. I just stood there dumbfounded. I couldn't believe I had missed anything so big so close. Once I regained my composure, I went over to the spot where the deer had been standing when I fired. There was enough blood in the snow to indicate a solid hit. I felt somewhat reassured of my marksmanship. I started out on the trail of the old buck's tracks, which were easy to follow in the snow, and it became evident that he was leaking worse than a '49 Hudson. I only had to follow the tracks about 100 yards to find my deer neatly stacked up in the snow under a big oak tree.

As I write this, that buck looks down at me from the wall of my den. He's a big symmetrical eight-pointer, and scores between 135 and 145 points by my unofficial measurements. And he owes his demise to a good stalk on my part that took the wind into account and some bad luck on his part. If it hadn't been so cold, I might have stayed on my stand a little longer and if so, would never have seen him.

Before leaving the subject of stalking, the importance of moving slowly must be reemphasized. Cover a small tract of land and cover it thoroughly. Stalking at a typical pace, 600 yards per hour, the hunter can cover 1,800 yards in three hours. In good deer country it is unlikely that you can go 1,800 yards without crossing paths with a fair-sized buck. But will you see him? Or will he see you first and slip away unnoticed? This type of hunting requires great patience and more stamina than you might at first suppose because it takes a lot of effort to move through the woods in a slow and deliberate fashion for long periods of time. If you get tired, pick a good place for a stand and rest for a while. You just might bag your buck while sitting under a tree resting. Lots of hunters have.

Tracking

When the sky darkens and the barometer drops during deer season, the hunter's pulse quickens with visions of a tracking snow. For all the attention that tracking receives in books and articles about deer hunting, it is surprising just how little of the time the ground conditions are suitable for it. By suitable for tracking, I mean suitable for tracking by the average hunter who, with a little luck, can distinguish between the tracks of a deer and a Volkswagen. The human bloodhounds who can stay on the trail of a deer strolling down a paved sidewalk are few and far between. Most of us need some help in the way of snow, since patches of soft ground are usually too limited in extent. In the last few seasons that I hunted in New York, there were a total of only two or three days when the snow conditions were such that extensive tracking was really possible. In more northern parts of the country, farther north in New York, in northern Vermont, in Maine and in much of the Northwest, good snow cover is usually available during most of the hunting season.

The most common way to track is to walk through the woods until a likely looking set of large tracks is found, and then to start following them. The idea is that if you are stealthy enough, you may actually sneak up on the deer, and even if you spook him you may still be lucky enough to get a shot. The deer seem to sense the added danger of the trail they leave behind them in the snow, so they are particularly careful when snow is on the ground. They watch their back trail carefully and circle around frequently to see if they are being followed. The tracker can use a similar ploy by observing the direction in which the tracks appear to be going and trying to intercept them at some point ahead by taking a short cut or cresting over a ridge line.

One problem with following tracks in this manner is that the hunter may come to the end of a long day of careful tracking only to find a large, well-fed doe standing in the tracks he has been following all day. One way to avoid this unhappy turn of events is to wait until you jump a buck by just walking through the woods and then start following what you know are a set of male tracks. The disadvantage of this method is that such a deer will know from the outset that he is being followed and will make every effort to shake his pursuers. There are, however, some hunters who make a habit of picking up a set of tracks and sticking to it like glue on the theory that sooner or later the deer will get careless or get curious about what's following him and he will expose himself long enough to give the hunter the opportunity for a shot. Most hunters who use this method expect, or at least hope, that the opportunity for a shot will present itself somewhere in the course of one day of tracking. But in the last few years there have been filtering out of the hills of Vermont stories of a new breed of deer hunters who have developed this technique to a fine art and whose deer always dress out at 200 pounds or more. Needless to say, these stories have left the rest of the hunting fraternity at something of a loss for words.

The hunters who use this new technique attack a set of tracks with a vengeance. They pick up the trail one day and stick to it—for ten or twenty miles if necessary. The next day they pick it up again and follow it in the same dogged manner. This usually goes on for anywhere from one to ten days—up hills, down mountainsides, and across valleys—until finally the hunter gets the shot for which he has worked so long and so hard. The glowing accounts indicate an extremely high success probability for this technique with excellent odds of getting a big rack.

Offsetting the alleged effectiveness of this method are certain obvious drawbacks. In the first place, most folks don't have ten consecutive days to spend hunting deer. Secondly, after two days of hiking twenty miles per day through foot-deep snow in the mountains of Rutland County, Vermont, where I used to live, most of the hunters whom I know would be stretcher cases. Finally, it takes an exceptionally good tracker to stick to the same set of tracks for several consecutive days, even under good snow conditions. The deer will become more and more determined to shake the tracker as he is pursued longer and longer. He will circle back, backtrack, walk with other deer, and use heavily traveled runways. He will walk through streams and swamps which may or may not be frozen over. Sometimes the tracker will swear that he must have sprouted wings. But if you have the time, stamina, and tracking ability, this type of dogged pursuit may pay off in big dividends for you. Sooner or later, even the smartest old buck will get careless.

Floating

As was pointed out in Chapter 3, whitetail deer are fond of the water and show a decided liking for certain species of water plants. If not molested, deer can often be found in the early morning and late afternoon along the margins of lakes and streams in search of various gastronomic delights. Deer in such situations show little predisposition to expect danger from the water, and if the wind direction is right, the hunter in a boat stands a good chance of drifting to within gunshot range.

There are several other advantages of float-hunting. If the area being hunted is remote but accessible by boat, the boat makes

11–3 The float hunter's boat does more than just provide an effective platform from which to hunt. In many cases the boat also saves hours of backbreaking work in hauling the game out of the woods. (Courtesy of Ontario Ministry of Industry and Tourism)

for easy transportation of the carcass. In areas where growth along the shoreline is thick, it may be difficult to stalk in close enough or to find a stand with adequate visibility for a good hunt of the shoreline. Floating also facilitates the examination of lots of terrain in a short time. By simply drifting around the end of a point of land, the hunter with a pair of binoculars may find from 500 to 1,000 yards of shoreline around a cove or inlet exposed to his view.

The best craft for floating is the canoe, and this is particularly true if the hunter is planning to hunt alone. The canoe can easily be managed by one man with his rifle close by. The canoe also allows the hunter to face the direction of travel, and this is an obvious advantage. If two men are hunting together, the man in the back can paddle while his partner sits up front at the ready. John-boats and rowboats can be used by two hunters, one rowing while the other hunts; or they can be adapted to solo hunting by the addition of an electric outboard. These motors are quiet enough that they do not bother the deer, and the motor is off much of the time when float hunting anyway. These motors can also be used effectively on square-stern canoes. Before using any type of watercraft for deer hunting, be sure to check your local game laws, since there are restrictions on their use in some areas.

While the sound of the electric motor does not seem to bother deer, other strange noises will put them to flight. While bugging for bass, I have motored up so close to deer wading in a pond that I could have swatted them across their bottoms with my cane pole. But let the butt of the pole rap against the bottom of the boat, and off they go in a churning watery blur mixed with mud, water lilies, and white flags. To avoid the possibility, soundproof your craft as much as possible. A thick piece of old carpet laid in the bottom of the boat is a good start. A split piece of garden hose slipped over the gunwales will help keep paddles from rapping against the side of the boat. Find a silent, secure, padded place to put your rifle and binoculars, and make sure that any extraneous gear is well secured.

Besides looking for deer wading in the water, try floating in close enough to the shore to look for deer traveling along the trails that so often parallel shorelines and stream banks. These trails are usually anywhere from five to thirty yards from the shore, and the deer using them will not be expending great amounts of effort watching the water for signs of danger.

There are some disadvantages to floating. As mentioned above, it is illegal in some areas. It is also no mean trick to accurately place a shot from a rocking watercraft, so you may actually have to step onto the bank for your shot. In areas where the hunting pressure is heavy, the deer are not likely to expose themselves by feeding in lakes during daylight hours. The technique is probably most applicable to the remote areas of national forests and large commercially held tracts. But where it is applicable, float-hunting provides a pleasant blend of wilderness camping, deer hunting, and maybe even a little fishing on the side. What more could any man ask from life?

12

Driving

Of the approximately two-and-a-half million whitetail deer shot in this country last year, it is estimated that 20 percent to 40 percent of them were taken on deer drives. While the drive does not provide the individual challenge and sense of accomplishment that one gets from a successful stalk, it is one of the best ways for the novice to become familiar with the sport, and under certain terrain conditions it is the only practical way to hunt deer.

Drive Organization

In a typical drive, somewhere between six and fifteen hunters combine forces. Some of the hunters will be designated as drivers, and they will form a line and move through an area suspected of harboring deer. The other hunters will be designated as standers, and they are stationed in advance along the escape routes that it is expected the deer will follow as they move before the advancing line of hunters.

This seems like a fairly straightforward matter, but it requires careful advance preparation and organization. If the drive is to be successful, it must be directed by one man who is usually called the drive captain. The captain will determine the positions to be taken by the standers and the route of advance of the drivers. This requires extensive knowledge of the area to be hunted, likely locations of deer at different times of the day, and probable avenues of escape of the deer.

One of the most important responsibilities of the drive captain is safety. In particular, the possibility of a stander shooting a driver or of a driver shooting another driver must be eliminated. In some hunting groups, the drivers are not permitted to carry guns, or else only the hunters on the end of the line of drivers are armed. If the drivers are armed, they must fully understand the importance of shooting only to the front or to the rear. Shots to either side along the line of drivers are dangerous. One way to keep control is to issue the men on either end of the line crow calls and have them alternate "caws" every few minutes. Don't try to cover too wide an area, and try to keep each driver in visual contact with the driver to his right and left. Another good safety device is to place the standers in elevated stands so they are shooting down at the deer and hence don't endanger the drivers.

Don't try to make the drive too long. A number of shorter drives will usually pay bigger dividends, and the shorter drives are easier to control. Deer resist being driven very far from their home haunts, and it is very unlikely that you will be able to drive them as far as a mile before they circle around the line or slip back between the drivers. In most places, drives from 300 yards to half a mile are best. The shorter drives also permit more frequent changeover between drivers and standers. The changeover is traditionally made after each drive; it gives the standers a chance to warm up and stretch cramped muscles and gives the drivers a chance to rest.

Newly formed driving groups tend to use too many drivers and too few standers. The relative number of drivers and standers will vary from drive to drive depending on terrain and cover, but from one-half to two-thirds of the party on-stand for any given

12-1 A well-organized drive can be effective in many situations. The standers must get to their positions via some route that does not disturb the area to be driven. Between half and two-thirds of the hunting party should be on stand in a typical drive situation. It does not take many drivers to keep the deer moving.

drive is a good average. It doesn't take a whole regiment of hunters to make a big woodland ruckus, and a deer is quite easily intimidated by one man. But it takes a lot of alert standers to cover all the exits. In a party of ten, four drivers and six standers would be a good split.

An exception to the above rule concerning the split between drivers and standers is the power drive. The power drive is a technique that most hunters never use, and it is mentioned here simply as a matter of interest. This drive employs from thirty to as many as one hundred drivers and may sweep an area as large as a square mile. Sometimes no standers are posted at all and hunters rely on deer trying to slip through the line of hunters rather than circle it because the line is so long. Hunters who spot a deer slipping through the line must wait until the deer is through and behind the line of hunters to ensure a safe shot. Community drives such as this were once commonplace in, for example, the Pine Barrens of New Jersey. There the vegetation is thick, the ground is as flat as a pancake, and you could stumble over a deer before seeing him. Be sure to check on local game laws before trying to organize a power drive since some states limit the number of hunters that can participate in a drive.

Certain types of terrain lend themselves particularly well to drives. Islands in lakes and rivers can often be very effectively driven by a line of drivers spanning the entire width of the island. In some areas, peninsulas sticking out into lakes and rivers can be driven. In both cases be watchful for deer swimming to safety. Sometimes swamps can be efficiently driven. Some years ago, I used to hunt in an area in Orange County, New York, that had the fairly open mixed hardwood-and-conifer cover that is typical of much of that part of the country. But in a mountain depression, at an elevation of about 1,200 feet, there is a swamp so thick that three moose and an abominable snowman could be living in there and go undetected. The swamp is about 300 yards wide, half a mile long, and is wadable in most places. On one side of the swamp there is a steep rocky hill several hundred feet high with a heavily used runway running along its base. On the other side of the swamp is a well-defined logging road with enough clearing along its shoulders to provide good visibility. If I ever hunt that area again, I am going to organize a drive through the swamp to provide a little excitement for those big racks that I am sure hole up in there. Standers will be posted along the logging road, the runway at the base of the hill, and at the far end of the swamp where the trails leading from the swamp disappear into heavy rhododendron growth. A line of drivers in hip boots or knee-highs should be able to sweep the area clean if they are careful to hit every thicket and clump of high grass as they proceed. Who knows, maybe as I write this a new world-record head is bedded down on one of the little high and dry grassy mounds that dot the swamp. Or maybe he's curled up at the base of a hemlock listening to the robust bullfrog chorus that can be heard in the swamp every spring. But whatever that buck may be up to, I sure would like to make his acquaintance some fall.

Drivers

Novice hunters usually feel that being a stander during a drive is a stroke of good luck since the standers are more likely to get shots at deer. The more experienced hunter knows better. The alert driver has excellent chances of getting a shot if he is watchful for deer trying to slip through the line of drivers or trying to circle the end of the line. It is not at all unusual for the drivers to get more deer than the standers.

As stated previously, for safety reasons I like to see drivers maintain visual contact with the drivers to their right and left. Spacing close enough together to maintain visual contact also reduces the possibility of a deer slipping past the drivers. Obviously, then, the actual spacing between drivers is going to vary depending on how dense the vegetation is. In open woods, drivers 100 yards apart may be able to cover the area adequately. In heavy cover, fifty yards is probably too far apart.

Some groups like to have their drivers move through the woods making as much noise as possible. They shout and whistle, and some even carry artificial noisemakers or beat on pans. This always seemed like the wrong approach to me. I don't think that all that noise is necessary to frighten the deer and keep them moving. I have found that I can frighten the wits out of any deer in town by just walking through the woods in my normal ground-shaking, twig-snapping manner. In fact, I spook more deer than I care to admit when I'm stalking and making a deliberate and conscientious effort to be quiet. If each driver is making a big racket, it is easier for the deer to pinpoint the exact location of the drivers and to slip between them. If, however, the drivers are moving through the woods in a fairly quiet manner, it is more difficult for the deer to tell where each hunter is. The deer will know it is being pursued and will probably know there is more than one hunter. But if the line advances quietly, the deer are more apt to be kept off balance and moving forward. The quietly moving line will also panic the deer less frequently, thus giving the standers shots at more slowly moving targets.

Standers

Standers must be in position before the drive starts and must have a route selected that will get them to their stands without disturbing the area through which the drive is to be conducted. Standers should be stationed where they can observe all major runways and escape routes leading out of the drive area. Where possible, it is a good idea to drive the deer toward some open area, such as a log-

12–2 Drivers must be alert for deer trying to slip through the line of drivers. For safety's sake, drivers must also be alert at all times to insure that they know where the other drivers are. (Courtesy of Maine Fish and Game Dept. Tom Carbone)

ging road or a power-line clearing, that provides the standers with good visibility. The open area serves as a barrier that temporarily stops the deer. They will move up to the opening and stop in the last bit of cover to look for danger. As often as not, they will then bolt across the opening so fast that the hunter on stand will have little time for a shot. The stander should be stationed so he can see from ten to fifteen yards into the wood line or bush line to make possible shots at those deer contemplating the opening and trying to decide what to do.

Don't try to drive deer upwind to the standers. Even though they are being driven, the deer will not allow themselves to be forced into a line of standers if they smell them. They will become doubly evasive and make greater efforts to slip by the drivers. Furthermore, if they know by scent where the standers are, there is a better chance that they can get by the standers unobserved.

It is also taboo for the stander to move from his position until either the line of drivers has passed or he is relieved by the drive captain. The position of each stander is selected to contribute to the overall effect of the hunt and the stander must not move even if he gets his deer. Stay in position. In some states the stander is allowed two deer. So stay put.

Some hunters participating in drives as standers get careless and move and fidget more than they would if they were stand-hunting alone. Don't fall into this trap. The technique of standing described in Chapter 10 is just as applicable to standers on a drive as it is to the solo hunter. Select your stands carefully, camouflage them, and be as still as possible. Some hunters think it is all right, for example, to smoke on stand because the smell of cigarette and campfire smoke does not alarm deer. It is not the smoke itself that alarms the deer, it is all the associated movement of lighting, puffing, raising the cigarette, and lowering it again.

Driving with Dogs

In much of the southeastern United States and in the Canadian province of Ontario, it is legal to hunt deer with dogs. The usual method is to use the dogs in place of the human drivers and to station a line or lines of stand hunters as is done with ordinary driving. To those Yankees unfamiliar with this type of hunting, this may seem like a singularly unsporting way to go about collecting venison. There are, however, two sides to this story. In the first place, the swamps and thickets in the parts of the country where this method is commonly employed are so thick that even the rabbits get lost. It would be impossible in such cover to maintain a safely organized line of drivers. Furthermore, there are difficulties associated with this type of hunting that may not at first be apparent and which serve to make hunting deer with dogs more difficult than it sounds. Picture the difficulty of maintaining control of a pack of black-and-tan hounds crashing full tilt through the briars and brambles hot on the trail of a buck heading for the state line. The hounds as often as not don't know when they've passed the line of standers; and if the stander doesn't stack that buck up neat as cordwood as he goes by, those hounds may chase that venison clear to the Gulf of Mexico.

Quite aside from the practical aspects of hound-hunting deer, there is the matter of tradition. Hounding deer is an ancient sport that, like hunting foxes with hounds, dates back to medieval England. Henry VIII (1491–1547) is known to have kept a pack of staghounds, and the practice no doubt predates his time. When the English colonists came to this country, they brought with them

12–3 In the southeastern United States, hunting deer with hounds is considered an ancient and honorable sport. In places where such hunting is practiced, mixed-breed packs are the rule rather than the exception. (Courtesy of Virginia Commission of Game and Inland Fisheries)

their traditional hunting methods, or more correctly, the traditional hunting methods of the British upper classes.

The first dogs used on deer in this country were probably retrained foxhounds. As time passed and American breeds were developed, such breeds as Walkers, redbones, blueticks, black-and-tans, and beagles became popular for hunting deer. It should be pointed out, though, that there has never been developed in this country a "deer hound" that was bred and trained just for deer. Mixed-breed packs are more popular than pedigree packs, and most deer hunters look for results in a hound and don't worry too much about pedigree since most deer won't stop a hound and ask it for its papers anyhow. Deer packs consist of all manner of mixes of the above breeds, and one even sees crossbreeds of such unlikely breeds as German shepherds and Irish setters. Some are so nondescript as to be termed only pure dog.

A good deer hound should obviously be disciplined and

have a good nose. It might seem that stamina would also be a desirable quality, but this works against the hunter more often than it works for him. For example, Walkers are big, wide-ranging dogs. When they get on a trail, nothing short of the Mississippi River will stop them, and it is not unusual for a pack owner to be out well after dark bugling in a pack of Walkers that ran some frisky buck fifteen miles into the next parish. The redbone is also a big, wide-ranging dog, and if you don't shoot the deer being chased by a pack of redbones, one drive may be all you get for the day.

The black-and-tan is a slimmed-down model of the bloodhound, and is reputed to have the best nose of all deer dogs. This breed is a little smaller than either the Walker or the redbone and is somewhat easier to control. In either purebreds or crossbreeds, this is a popular dog. The bluetick is even smaller, but has outsized endurance for such a small beast; and it may take you five days and three counties to collect your pack of blueticks after a good hard chase.

In recent years, the beagle has grown tremendously in popularity. Because of his small size, the beagle can penetrate through thick brush that would stop or slow up the larger dogs. Also, because of his small size and limited endurance, the beagle is more likely to call it quits after a chase and return to the driver's call. Another advantage of the smaller dog is that it does not press the deer as hard and the standers are more apt to get a shot at a walking or trotting deer. You've never seen a deer in high gear until you've seen one being pursued by a pack of big Walkers in a sight chase. When the dogs have the deer in sight, the barking comes at closer intervals, the adrenaline flows faster, and the pace is frantic. The deer pulls out all the stops and turns into a brown blur that is harder to hit than a two-inch x-ring at 1,000 yards.

Hounding deer is a whole different experience for the hunter who tries it. It is a social way of hunting, usually done in clubs of fifteen to twenty members on land leased from plantation owners or forest companies. It is a way of hunting steeped in tradition and practiced in this country since colonial times and in England before that. It is a way of hunting that combines the usual drive hunter's satisfaction with the upland bird hunter's satisfaction of working with well-trained dogs. The hound hunter associates the smells of brewing coffee, gunpowder, and the autumn woods with his sport as do other deer hunters. But for him the experience would be incomplete without the distant music of a pack of hounds on the trail of a fresh scent.

13

Special Hunting
Methods

The hunting methods and techniques described up to
this point are very general and may be employed anywhere. There are other specialized techniques that are
not so general in their applicability, but they are, nonetheless, important additions to the hunter's repertoire of
hunting skills. This chapter treats several subjects
which may be just what the doctor ordered for some
special hunting situations.

Hunting Arid Country

A whitetail deer hunter in the arid southwest is confronted with a somewhat different situation from hunters in the North and the Southeast. The arid semidesert climates of such states as Texas, New Mexico, and Arizona present temperature and terrain situations unique to the area. But the same basic hunting principles apply, and the accomplished whitetail deer hunter of the North will, with a little adjustment, do well in this part of the country.

In this area, where whitetail and mule deer ranges often overlap, the two animals provide an interesting contrast in relative cunning. The mule deer tends to be a more trusting, less alert, and more easily stalked animal. But the whitetail deer in this area, like the whitetail everywhere, is cunning to an extreme. He'll slip down a dry-wash creek bed on you, and he'll use every little bush and cactus for cover in a nearly barren piece of land. Sometimes you'll swear he could hide behind a single blade of grass. And like his Northern and Eastern cousins, his guard is almost never down.

The terrain in these semiarid regions is typically rocky with vegetation ranging from sparse grass and cactus to thick cover of mesquite and thornbush. The area is often gullied with dry-wash creek beds that don't even remotely resemble creeks except immediately after a rain—at which time they resemble raging torrents. The weather during hunting season is much warmer than that typically associated with the Northern season and it may not even be cold enough to initiate the rut. Since the weather change is less dramatic, the rut tends to be more diffuse and stretches over a longer period. In a given area, the rut may begin in September with bucks still seen pursuing does in late January.

The daily movement patterns of deer under such circumstances are different from those in cooler, moister climes. Yet the same basic factors, pursuit of food and water, comfort, and safety (and does during the rut) are the primary determinants of the deers' movements. During the heat of the day, the deer try to move as little as possible and stay out of the sun. Whitetails will move down into the dry creek beds, look for the thickest vegetation possible, and curl up to wait out the sun. A good way to hunt under such circumstances is to stalk along the bank of the creek beds with a pair of binoculars to examine carefully the creek bottom. An occasional stone thrown into the creek bed will often cause startled motion from deer that would otherwise have gone undetected. Adept snapshooters will sometimes stalk upwind right through the creek bed itself, but this method usually calls for some lightning-fast shooting in heavy brush.

Stalking and trail watching are the two most common methods of hunting such areas, but drives are sometimes used in especially heavy cover. The tandem stalking method is particularly good for hunting the clumps of heavy brush. A solo hunter tromping through such brush would find that the deer simply exit from the far side, circle back, and reenter the brush behind him. When two men hunt together, one goes through the brush and the other circles around to intercept escaping deer. Two stalkers can also be effective hunting the banks of a dry wash with one hunter on each bank to intercept deer scrambling up either side.

Trail watching is difficult in some areas because of the difficulty of spotting runways on the rocky ground. Because of the openness of the terrain, the deer tend to spread out over a larger area and the runways are not well-defined except in heavy brush where the paths are more clearly delineated. Certain generalizations can, however, be made concerning how the animals will move. In going from beds to feeding and watering areas and vice versa, whitetails will take advantage of every scrap of cover and will make every effort to avoid exposing themselves. In leaving a brushy area, if a finger of brush protrudes from the clump, they will walk as far out into the finger as possible before leaving the cover and they will enter the first such projection sticking out of the next brushy area. Along the way they will walk through, or adjacent to, every conceivable piece of cover in a manner furtive enough to make a superspy envious.

Deer in the North and Southeast almost always have an abundance of water. Such is not always the case in the arid areas. A whitetail deer requires two to three quarts of water a day for each hundred pounds of body weight. This much water is not always easy to come by, hence water-hole stands can sometimes prove worthwhile.

Storm Fronts

I have already made frequent allusions to the importance of weather in the hunter's strategy. The deer react to the weather and the hunter must adjust his methods accordingly. Rain, snow, unseasonable heat, and the like all have their effect on deer. But this effect is most dramatic and noticeable when the weather is changing, especially when a storm is coming in or going out.

I can recall a fall in the early 1960s when I was doing some preseason scouting high on a ridge line in Rutland County, Vermont. It had been clear and cold all day when suddenly about three o'clock in the afternoon it started to cloud over and the sky turned gray. Within fifteen minutes the sky turned from gray to pitch black, and it was obvious that the hills were in for a bit of a blow. The temperature plummeted 10 degrees once the sun disappeared; and the November woods, somber enough in broad daylight, became downright ominous. The wind began to stiffen and become skittish, shifting this way and that. I was sitting on a high bluff overlooking a saddle a quarter of a mile wide and several hundred yards deep when nature played a strange weather prank as she so often does along storm fronts. Even though the bluff that I was standing on was at an elevation of only 2,400 feet, I all at once found that I was looking down at puffy white clouds slipping through the saddle below me. I pulled out my binoculars to watch the meteorological phenomenon more closely since I don't often get to look down at clouds while standing on the ground. I suddenly realized that the saddle below me had come alive with deer that were wandering all over it. They didn't appear to be going anywhere in particular, mind you, just wandering. The saddle quickly became socked in with swirling snowy clouds, and I found myself looking down at a snowstorm for the first time in my life. The reverie was short lived, though, for within minutes the whole bluff was engulfed in a blustery swirling sea of snowflakes. This snow was the first significant snow of the year, and as I staggered and stumbled the two miles back to camp I saw more deer drifting about aimlessly in those woods than I had previously thought lived in the whole county. In fact, the deer activity had been unusually high all day long — even in the middle of the day.

There have been many reasons given for the increased activity of deer just before and just after a storm. Some say that deer can sense the dropping barometer and head out to stock up on groceries before they get snowed or rained in and are forced to miss a few meals. Others say that the first snow of the season is a disconcertingly new and strange phenomenon for the short-memoried deer, and it confuses them and makes them uneasy. I have watched deer gamboling around as the first flakes of a storm fell for what seemed to be the fun of playing in the snow. In some cases, such as this one in Vermont where the deer are caught between beds and feeding areas by a sudden storm of unusual severity, I don't doubt that that storm confuses them. It confused me at times as I was heading back to camp, and I was raised in those hills.

The motivation for movement after the storm is a little more obvious. Cramped muscles need to be exercised, and empty paunches need a refill. The stalker will find that the day after a drenching rainstorm is excellent for hunting. The ground is damp, and leaves and twigs are silenced. Moist spots are abundant and tell a tale of tracks made since the rain stopped. And, best of all, old whitey will be up and moving about.

Unfortunately, the termination of a heavy snowstorm does not always initiate a similar burst of activity. If the snow is heavy enough, deer will be reluctant to get up and plow through it. Rather, they will be content to sit and wait for a few days, moving as little as possible, and hoping someone else will perform the energy-consuming task of plowing the first path through the snow. But if the snow is not too heavy, increased activity can be expected immediately following termination of the storm.

Wounded Deer

The best advice I can give any hunter concerning wounded deer is don't wound any. Reread Chapter 4 on marksmanship, take those lessons to heart, and you, I hope, will never have to spend a day trying to run down a crippled deer. And make no mistake about it, if you wound one, its your job to track it down. In the late 1940s, my family owned a small spread of several hundred acres in Vermont. I can still recall how distressing it was for me as a youngster to go out into the woods and find the remains of cripples that had died after being hit. Some of the deer were antlerless animals that some "sportsman" had shot without waiting for positive identification. These misidentified animals were then just left to rot in our woods. On at least one occasion, though, I found a buck that the hunter was apparently unable to locate after shooting it. (All this land was, by the way, posted; no one was supposed to be hunting on it.) In my opinion, the second greatest sin that a hunter can commit is taking a careless shot at a deer. The worst thing that he can do is to fail to follow aggressively the trail of a deer that he has wounded whether his shot was careless or not.

A surprising number of deer shot by hunters are lost even though they drop within 200 yards of where the deer was hit. Even a deer hit with a well-placed, fatal shot will sometimes travel from fifty to 200 yards before piling up. And the more excited the deer is when he is hit, the more likely he is to travel. Adrenaline has amazing sustaining abilities. I have seen a frightened buck travel sixty yards after being hit, totally oblivious to the fact that he was missing half his heart. Farm boys that have had the job of chopping off the heads of a few chickens for the family supper are familiar with the bizarre sight of a decapitated chicken running madly around the yard. Motor mechanisms have a funny way of remaining active long after they have any reason to do so.

There are several things you can do immediately after firing to help preclude the loss of your deer. First, bring your head up right away to where you have a good view of where the deer was standing and at the same time be chambering another round just in case. A mortally hit deer will often flop and flounder for a few feet after being hit. If you are reasonably sure of your first shot in such circumstances, don't put a second round in him. You'll just ruin good venison. If the deer shows any inclination to run or sustain movement and you can fire a second shot, even if it's hasty and not carefully aimed, by all means do so. The next thing to do is to note carefully the position where the deer seemed to be standing when you fired. When you climb down out of your stand and run 150 yards to where you think the deer was, your perspective changes drastically. The deer could have dropped in place, but if you are twenty yards off that spot in heavy cover, you may not see him.

A solidly hit deer, even if he subsequently gets up, usually drops from the sheer impact of absorbing between 1,000 and 2,000 foot-pounds of bullet energy. But there are other indications of a hit. The injured deer will often drop his head and amble off with an unsteady gait. Some say that the deer will hunch over slightly and recoil a bit at the moment of bullet impact. Note that the moment of impact is essentially the same as the moment of firing. In my experience, the only thing hunching, recoiling, and recovering at the moment of firing is me. If you can squeeze a round off in a .30/06 and recover from the recoil and blast fast enough to verify the deer's behavior at bullet impact, your reflexes are so good that you probably keep dry in thundershowers by running between the raindrops.

If the deer continues to travel after you shoot, carefully note the spot where he disappeared from view and the direction he was heading. Then proceed to that point and start looking for a trail. If the hit was good and solid, a short walk in the general direction of the deer's departure will usually reveal him neatly stacked up nearby. If the hit was not as solid as it should have been, start looking for a trail. Even if you find no blood or tufts of hair, you should try to follow the animal for 150 or 200 yards or more to be sure it was a clean miss. But if you were confident enough of your shot to take it in the first place, you should have at least hit the animal.

Some hunters recommend waiting up to thirty minutes for the deer to bleed and stiffen up before getting on his trail. I don't. At least go check immediately the area where the animal was hit and the first few hundred yards of the trail. The shot will sometimes stun or temporarily disable the deer, thus providing the hunter with the opportunity for a quick finishing shot. If this opportunity is bypassed, the alternative may be a long and arduous trailing job after the deer has recovered his senses and taken flight.

In the absence of snow or soft earth, the tracking job can be quite difficult, especially if the deer is not bleeding profusely. Start at the point of impact and move out slowly in the direction of flight looking for telltale drops of blood. If you lose the trail, mark the place where you last spotted blood and walk in increasing con-centric circles about that point looking for new signs. As you pro-ceed, don't keep your eyes glued to the ground. Pause frequently and look up. You may just spot your quarry skulking off ahead of you. A pair of binoculars may be helpful. Keep glassing the area ahead looking for the piece of antler or patch of hair that will give away the position of your deer who may well be bedded down and resting.

If the trail just seems to give out, it's a good general rule that wounded deer will tend to travel downhill since it takes less effort. The most common exception to this rule is the deer hit in one of the front legs. Such an animal finds downhill going difficult be-cause he has only one good front leg on which to support the bulk of his body weight, which shifts to the front when going downhill. Another exception is the deer who is traveling downhill, is shot, and spots the hunter below him or to one side. Such a deer will try to turn around and go back up the hill.

Slingshots

Have you ever tried using slingshots on deer? The idea probably sounds crazy until you realize that the slingshot is not used to shoot at the deer. Rather, the projectile from the slingshot is used to scare the deer out of cover and toward the hunter. The technique is useful, especially for solo hunters, when a clump of heavy brush is encountered. It is virtually impossible for the lone hunter to get a smart buck who is holed up in such undergrowth. As the hunter penetrates the brush, the deer stays just far enough ahead to stay out of sight and circles back or slips into the next thicket or down the hillside. A few pebbles fired from a slingshot to the far side of the thicket and then a few more fired into the center of it may bring forth a sudden burst of hooves, tail, and antlers right into the hunter's sights.

This use of a slingshot is just a refinement of the age-old technique of throwing stones into the brush to frighten out game. The slingshot, however, works much better. For one thing, a good slingshot can cast a pebble or steel ball up to 200 yards, depending on the quality of the slingshot and the weight of the projectile. Sev-eral projectiles can easily be fired simultaneously, and there is no need for a lot of eye-catching motion as would be the case if the stones were thrown by hand.

To be most effective, the slingshot trap must be sprung in

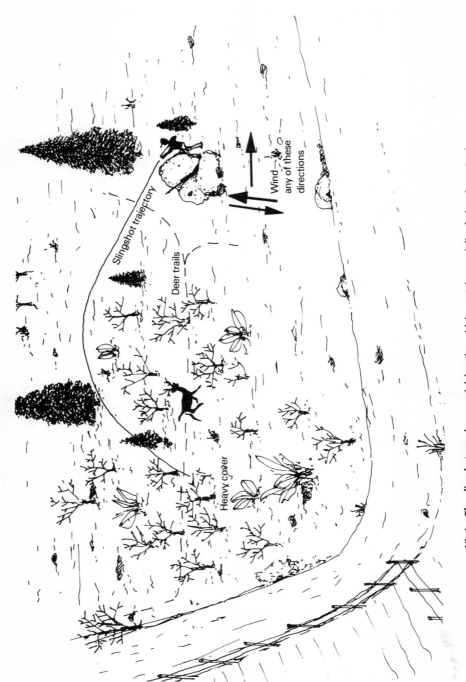

13-1 The slingshot can be a useful hunting aid in certain specialized situations. Begin by making a commotion on the far side of the cover. This will make the deer nervous. Then drop a few stones into the middle of the cover and there's a good chance that the deer will move out of the cover toward you.

two parts. Suppose you come upon a small, thick, swampy area about 100 yards in diameter. The first part of the trap consists of alerting deer to the possible presence of danger on the side of the swamp opposite from where you want them to come out. There are two ways to do this. One is to actually make some commotion on one side of the swamp yourself. This can be done by talking in low tones or by just walking around in infantry style. Then slip quietly to the far side of the cover. The initial disturbance will not be enough to scare a smart old buck out of cover where he feels safe. On the other hand, the commotion followed by ten to fifteen minutes of silence will make him nervous. This is just what you want. Once you are in a good position on the far side of the swamp and can observe the most likely escape routes, fire a few pebbles from your slingshot to the far side of the swamp—the side where you made the initial disturbance. This will get that old buck up on his feet. Then rattle a few into the middle of that swamp and out he'll come. The other way to cause the far-side disturbance is to just fire a few shots across the swamp and then wait ten or fifteen minutes before proceeding. This will often do the job, but it is not as effective as talking or walking on one side of the thicket to be hunted.

In an emergency, such as when a trophy buck is seen disappearing into some brush, this method can be used by the bow hunter. Take the worst arrow from your quiver, shoot to the far side of the thicket, and hope for the best. This method can cost you a fortune in lost arrows, but in any sort of emergency it could make the difference.

Good slingshots are available from two dollars to five dollars, and steel balls can be obtained in most big hardware stores for those disinclined to use pebbles. If you want to make your own slingshot, any even hardwood fork will do. The rubbers can be made from surgical tube split lengthwise with a razor blade, or they can be bought commercially made. The rubbers are best attached to the handle by wrapping them once around the handle and binding them off with medium-gauge monofilament fishing line. The pouch is fashioned from a piece of leather.

With a few minutes of practice, you will develop enough skill to be able to estimate ranges accurately enough for the purpose of driving deer. A little additional practice will enable you to drop bunnies and grouse for the camp stewpot in areas where slingshot hunting of small game is permitted. In any event, you should find the slingshot a useful addition to your hunting bag of tricks since it effectively gives you several additional drivers to do your bidding on every hunt.

Calling, Rattling, and Scents

The use of calls in whitetail deer hunting is not very widespread. This general lack of acceptance is probably attributable to several factors. For one thing, there are many hunting techniques not utilizing calls which, properly employed, are very effective. Therefore, the hunter is not forced to learn how to use calls if he is not so inclined. In addition, it takes a fair amount of practice to become proficient with a call, and the neophyte scares away as many deer as he attracts. However, under certain circumstances, calling can be effective; and the savvy hunter would be well advised to be familiar with the technique.

Calling deer is an old Indian trick that is accomplished by imitating the bleat of a doe or fawn. The Indians made the sound orally or with blades of grass held between the thumbs. But if you are not an old Indian, I submit that this old Indian trick is best accomplished with any one of the commercial calls on the market. These calls are available from such companies as Herter, Sport-Lore, and Olt.

The call is most effective on does who apparently take the call to be the bleat of a fawn in distress. It is particularly effective during the fawning season and thus may be useful at that time of year to wildlife photographers. This is not to say that bucks won't answer a call. They will—especially the young curious ones. In fact, does are probably attracted as much by curiosity as by the urge to assist a fawn in distress.

A hunter who wishes to engage in calling should find himself a well-concealed spot that is not in the middle of a large open area. The concealment for the hunter is needed since calling, putting down the call, and picking up a gun (or camera) all involve some inevitable amount of movement. Also, the hunter can expect most deer to approach a call quite warily. The hunter should not conceal himself in the middle of an open area because deer are skittish about crossing open areas to begin with, and are even more skittish about it when approaching a call.

The caller should be careful not to overuse the call. One or two bleats given every fifteen minutes to half an hour is about right. It takes some practice to use the call properly, and Herter can provide a record with sample calls on it to get the beginner started. The sample calls on the record should serve as a good point of departure for your own experimentation.

Do not expect a deer to call back in answer. While this occasionally happens it is the exception rather than the rule. Expect deer to approach cautiously. They may try to circle downwind to get a whiff of what's making all the fuss. Calling is possible year round, and part of its value is that it gives the hunter an opportunity to study deer behavior year round.

While calling is a technique that is more likely to bring in a doe, rattling is a technique that is more likely to bring in a buck. In fact, does rarely respond to rattling. Rattling consists of simulating a fight between two bucks, and the simulation is accomplished by clashing two antlers together to make a noise similar to that produced by the clashing antlers of combatting bucks.

The best antlers to use are those of medium size, from eight-point or ten-point racks. By medium size, I mean those with maximum spreads from sixteen to twenty inches. An even number of points and symmetrical distribution are desirable to insure that when the antlers are clashed together, each point will have an opposing point to engage on the other antler. If you encounter difficulty finding such antlers and are reluctant to cut up any of your own trophies, try your local taxidermist. Taxidermists have a way of winding up with unclaimed wall hangings.

The brow tines usually get in the way on a set of antlers to be used for rattling, and they should be cut off. If any of the other points are too long to be easily managed, they can be cut back to about eight inches. Drill a hole through each antler just above the burl (that's where the antler hooks on to the deer), run one end of a twenty four-inch piece of rawhide through each hole and tie a knot in the rawhide. This makes the antlers easier to lug around. Next paint about 50 percent of both antlers with bright international orange paint. The idea of rattling is to fool some deer into thinking that two bucks are fighting, and not to fool some hunter. When carrying the antlers through the woods, I like to keep them completely concealed in a backpack or under a coat in spite of the orange paint. The reason for only painting 50 percent of the antlers is so they can be rubbed down once or twice each year with linseed oil to help keep them from drying out. By leaving part of the antler unpainted, you are assured that the antler will absorb the oil readily.

To rattle the antlers, the hunter holds one in his right hand and one in his left hand, simulating the way the deer wore them on his head. The antlers are then crashed together; once brought into contact, they are twisted and grated together. This process is repeated evey five or ten minutes. To further simulate the sounds of combat, some hunters rap the backs of the antlers on the ground to imitate hoofbeats, and rattle nearby bushes. Try raking the tines a little in nearby leaves and gravel. Just remember not to overdo it! A little noise carries a long way, and you should try to minimize movement since you never know when you are being watched.

Some hunters report incredible success with rattling. The results tend to be more dramatic than the results achieved with call-ing since the hunter who is rattling is trying to arouse the buck's instinct to defend his territory. Rut-crazed bucks have been known to come crashing right into the hunter's blind while the hunter was rattling. In fact, the action is often so fast that many hunters prefer to do their rattling with two men in the blind. One rattles and the other handles the gun.

Since rattling plays on the buck's instinct to defend his mat-ing territory, it is most effective during the rut. Look for the rubs and scrapes that indicate that some feisty old buck has staked out the area as part of his nuptial domain. Find some nearby con-cealment, and begin your rattling. Let that old buck think that some Johnnies-come-lately are fighting over his territory, and be prepared for action.

Scents can also be a useful aid to the hunter. I don't believe, as some people do, that scents are useful in attracting deer. I be-lieve that their value lies in helping mask the scent of the hunter. I realize that there are documented instances of bucks running with their noses to the ground frantically following the footsteps of a hunter who had doused his boots with a musk scent. I am con-vinced that such cases are rare exceptions. The most you should ex-pect from a scent is that it will help mask your human scent.

In addition to the commercial scents available, there are other ways to mask human scent. I have, for example, experimented

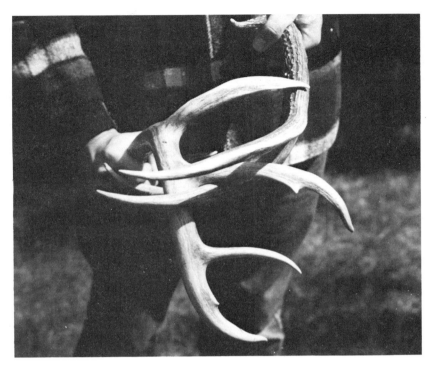

13–2 To rattle antlers for calling deer, begin by holding the antlers by the base in approximately the same relative positions as the deer wore them on his head. Then crash the antlers together. Next, twist the antlers to get a grating noise. Thump the ground occasionally but don't overdo. And be ready for action!

with hanging my clothes downwind of a smoky campfire. An hour or two of such a smoking will produce a not totally unpleasant, fairly long-lived aroma. If done each night on a camping trip, I expect that the practice has some merit. Some hunters bury their clothes in a heap of pine needles or dab pine pitch on their clothing. Others put their clothing in a box of cut-up apples and let them stand for a few days before the season begins. Needless to say, the added value of all this effort is hard to prove. I suspect that it has some value. I am more firmly convinced, however, that the best way to mask the human scent is to keep the deer upwind of you.

Part Four

The Trophy

14

Carcass and Trophy Care

Now let's assume that you have carefully followed all of the author's invaluable advice given in the preceding chapters. If you have done so, you are probably standing right now over a magnificent ten- or twelve-point buck that is a sure bet to place high on the Boone and Crockett listing. (If you are reading this in your living room, don't bother looking down at your feet; you get the idea.) The problem now is to convert that magnificent beast into table fare and a wall hanging.

Field Dressing

The first thing of which you have to be absolutely sure as you approach your downed deer is that he is actually dead. A deer that is only stunned or wounded can do some serious fighting back when you stick him with your knife to start the cleaning process. If he's still alive, you may be surprised at how determined he will be to retain possession of his innards a little longer.

When approaching a downed deer, approach cautiously, with a round in the chamber just in case. Either poke the animal with your rifle barrel or bow, or hit him with a stone from a few feet away. If there is no reaction, check the deer's eyes. If they have started to glaze or if they can be touched with a blade of grass with no reaction, the beast is quite dead. Avoid putting "insurance" shots into the carcass if at all possible. One well-placed shot from an adequate firearm is quite sufficient to kill a deer cleanly. Additional shots just ruin meat and hide. If a second shot is needed, I prefer a shot through the neck, rear to front, through the spinal column. If the head is to be mounted, place the shot sideways through the center of the ribcage instead. Placed here, the shot won't hit any viscera and will only ruin some spareribs which are of questionable value on most deer anyway. Most pundits who write of their deer-hunting experiences cite one or two cases (usually by name) of individuals who have been gored, slashed, kicked, or butted by deer that came to life as the hapless hunter went in with his knife to start cleaning. Sometimes the deer in question allegedly took off with the poor hunter's rifle dangling from his antlers. I can honestly say that none of my hunting companions is such a durn fool that he has ever let such a thing happen to him, and I have never even met a person who admitted to such an experience. But the possibility does exist; so step one of the field-dressing process must be *make sure the deer is dead*.

The next step in cleaning a deer is to calm down and recollect yourself after the excitement of the kill. While you are waiting for your adrenaline level to subside, take off your coat if you are wearing one, and roll up your sleeves. Whatever else field dressing large game may be, it is not neat; and you will have blood up to your elbows before you are done. And don't try to put off the field-dressing job, even for an hour or two, since it must be started right away to keep the meat from spoiling.

Roll the carcass over on its back with the head end slightly uphill. Using a short piece of string or excess shoelace, tie off the urinary tract. On a buck this involves no more than tying off the penis good and tight. On a doe, a circular incision must be made around the vaginal opening and then the opening should be pulled out slightly from the body cavity and tied off. This operation will make sure urine does not escape and taint the meat during the field-dressing procedure.

I generally dispense with two other preparatory steps that some authorities recommend. One is removal of the metatarsal glands on the inside of a buck's rear legs near the knee joint. These glands look like small tufted pads, and some feel that the excretion of these glands may taint the meat. I don't see much chance of the rear knee joint contacting the meat; and I expect that if the fluids from this gland can taint the meat, you run a greater risk of doing so by contaminating your knife and hands during the removal process than you do by simply leaving the gland alone to begin with. The other formality with which I dispense is the circular incisions around and the tying off of the anal opening. I have found that this is somewhat tricky to do properly on a deer; and that if the rest of the cleaning is done carefully, there is little chance of the feces contaminating the meat.

Next make a circular incision around the penis and free it from any attachment to the wall of the body cavity. Then make a straight cut from this circular incision rearward to a point as near the anus as possible. Then make another incision from the penis forward to the breastbone. In making all of these incisions through the wall of the body cavity, great care must be taken to avoid cutting any internal organs. In particular, avoid cutting the intestines or you run the risk of fouling the meat. To insure that you don't cut the internal organs, use the following procedure: place the first two fingers of the left hand inside the body cavity and lift the cavity wall up and away from the innards. Place the blade of your knife between these two fingers with the cutting edge up and cut from the inside out taking care not to puncture any organs with each forward thrust of the knife.

If the head is not going to be mounted, I prefer to split the breastbone and continue the belly cut forward to the base of the neck. If the head is to be mounted, stop the forward cut at the breastbone. If your knife is sharp and of adequate dimensions that the handle can be grasped with two hands, the breastbone can be split easily with the knife. Simply insert the knife into the body cavity behind the breastbone with the cutting edge up and lift with two hands while straddling the deer. The breastbone will then part readily.

At this point the entrails have to be loosened from the body cavity. This is done by reaching around and behind the organs with both hands and tearing the organs loose. In some cases a little assist from your knife, particularly around the diaphragm, is helpful. This is the operation for which you rolled up your sleeves!

This is the time to remove the heart and liver if you want them. It's a good idea to bring along a small plastic bag for the purpose of storing and carrying the heart, liver, and any other internal organs that you want to save. These organs have a way of turning into dirty, unpalatable messes around most hunting camps unless some special effort is made to protect them.

Now you can start wholesale removal of the remaining innards. If you have at hand a means to hoist the carcass off the ground head first, this is a good time to do so. Hoisting the carcass at this point will cause many of the organs to fall out or at least hang out to where they can be easily removed with a few strokes of the knife. If you have no readily available means to hoist the carcass, simply roll it over on its belly and shake or bounce it as best you can and most of the innards will shake loose.

Next, reach up to the throat as far as you can, pull down on the esophagus, and cut it. Then cut the intestine as close to the anal opening as possible. This can be done with little or no possibility of contaminating any meat if it is done carefully. Now comes the operation that makes it possible to clean the rear end of the carcass properly. Take your hatchet, a saw, or a good, heavy hunting knife and chop through the pelvic bone right in the middle. This operation is done much more easily with a hatchet than with a knife and this is one of the reasons why I recommend that every hunter either carry a lightweight hatchet with him or have one readily available to him back at camp. With the carcass lying on its back, several healthy blows with the hatchet should suffice to chop through the bone. Once this is done, the hindquarters will lay back flat on the ground making it much easier to perform any final cleaning operations and also making it easier to prop the carcass open for cooling. Trim out any remaining organs or loose attachments around the pelvis or in the body cavity. The carcass is now ready for transporting back to camp or to your car.

Transporting

Lugging a field-dressed deer out of the woods or back to the camp is definitely a job for two men if there is any distance involved. Typical field-dressed carcasses range in weight from ninety to 190 pounds, and getting them from point A to point B over rough terrain full of brush, with maybe a foot of snow on the ground, while packing a rifle and other miscellaneous gear is a challenging physical endeavor.

One way to accomplish the feat is simply to drag the deer out head first. Dragging has the advantage over carrying in that you don't have to lift the deer, you just provide the forward motive force. (Sounds easy, doesn't it?) If your specimen came supplied with a nice set of handle-bar antlers, you've even got a ready-made handle that can be grasped by one or two men for dragging. Don't worry about ruining the rack; those antlers are stronger than you think. One exception to this rule is a rack that is still in velvet. If you get a velvet rack that you want to preserve and have mounted, care must be taken not to damage the velvet. Don't try to drag such an animal by the antlers, and avoid scraping the antlers in transportation. If the deer you bagged was a doe or a spikehorn, built-in handles are missing and you must resort to other methods. In such cases, tie a rope around the animal's neck and use the rope to drag. Some hunters find it helpful to tie the other end of the rope to the center of a short, stout piece of tree limb and to use the piece of limb as a handle.

Dragging works fine on fairly smooth, level, or downhill terrain. If there is snow on the ground and the snow is not excessively deep and powdery, it works even better. However, rough terrain or uphill drags are tough. You drag one good-size buck up the steep sides of an arroyo or dry wash, and you'll wish you had brought your favorite pack horse along.

There are certain unconventional variations on dragging of which not everyone is aware. An example of such a variation is tobogganing. That's right, tobogganing. And I don't mean on a toboggan. I mean on the deer. Let me explain. Several years ago, I shot a big old buck high up on a moutainside in Virginia. After field dressing the critter, I dragged him about half a mile through the snow back to our camp, which was also high up on the mountain. My hunting partner and I broke camp, and he took all the gear, mine and his, and headed back down the mountain to the car, which was about one-and-a-half miles away. That left me with that old buck to transport out, and I was already pretty tired from dragging him back to camp in the first place. So I started down the mountain. Before long I was huffing and puffing, and my lungs were sure there was a local atmospheric oxygen deficiency. The antlers snagged on every bush, then the carcass would slide ahead in the snow, and then it would hang up on exposed rocks. My deer rifle felt like it weighed a ton. Then, when I was about to topple from exhaustion, I came to a relatively clear, snow-covered downhill stretch, and just as I expected, that carcass started to slip ahead of me. At that point I just threw dignity to the wind, flopped on top of my traveling companion, and together we went whizzing down the hill with friend deer serving as the toboggan. The rest of the way down that mountain, I took advantage of every opportunity that came along to ride instead of drag. I'm sure that big old buck and I presented a somewhat ridiculous picture sliding down the slopes, but as anyone who has ever dragged a deer knows, the state of utter exhaustion that such dragging induces quickly convinces one to accept minor compromises to his dignity.

Another disadvantage of dragging is that it is pretty easy to wear or poke holes in the hide, and if you want to have it tanned you are better off carrying your deer. One of the best ways to carry a deer is to lash it between two light poles. One hunter takes the front end with one pole on each shoulder and the other hunter takes the back end with one pole on each shoulder. The two-pole carry means carrying a little more weight than would be the case if only one pole were used, but it has two significant advantages. First, it distributes the weight onto both shoulders. With only one pole the shoulders quickly tire, and the pole tends to slip off. Second, two poles tend to eliminate the side-to-side swinging of the carcass, which can make the one-pole carry very difficult in rough terrain.

There are other ways to carry a deer out of the woods. Some hunters construct a *travois* out of light poles. The travois is a device shaped like an elongated letter A to which the deer is tied. The hunter then picks up the travois at the apex of the A and drags it out. In addition to the deer, the hunter's rifle and other gear can be tied to the travois. I have always found these devices to be rather heavy and awkward, but some fairly experienced hunters I know swear by them.

If the deer is not too big, and the other gear being transported is not too heavy or bulky, and if the terrain is not too rough, the deer can literally be picked up and carried out. This is usually accomplished by tying the front legs to the back legs as high up the legs as possible, typically around the knee joints. The hunter then passes his head and one arm through the opening between the deer's body and legs and slings the animal over his shoulder. The load usually rides easiest if the animal's legs are to the hunter's front and the chest and forequarters ride high on one shoulder. The obvious disadvantage of this method is that a deer being so carried out on a hunter walking through the woods could look somewhat like a deer without a hunter walking through the woods. If such a mistaken identification were to take place, both the hunter and his dead deer run the risk of receiving circular perforations of a ballistic origin. While I don't highly recommend this method, I have used it on several occasions myself and strongly recommend tying as much red and orange as possible to the deer's antlers, tail, and broadside.

I don't feel that an important and nostalgic part of my hunting experience consists of dragging the critter back to camp or the car. I would much rather be back at the camp with my deer hanging from the meat pole, a hot plate of hash smothered in ketchup in front of me, and be recounting between mouthfuls the details of the hunt to all those unfortunates who *obviously* don't know the first thing about deer hunting. Since I place a low value on the character-building experience of dragging the deer out, I fully support the use of all mechanical or beastly means of assistance in getting the kill back to camp. If you can get your deer out with a pack horse, snowmobile, boat, trail bike, four-wheel-drive vehicle, or any other form of transportation, by all means do so.

Once you get your deer back to your vehicle, the trek home begins. The best place to transport the carcass is usually on the roof of your car or on top of the trunk lid, provided the sun is not too hot. If the road is dusty, wrap the carcass in cheesecloth to protect it. Trunks are acceptable if propped open slightly for air circulation. The problem with trunks is that they have a tendency to get dusty inside on dirt roads, and often exhaust fumes will collect in the trunk. This is true even with the trunk lid closed, especially on older cars the trunks of which are usually no longer airtight. In foul weather I have transported deer in the back of a station wagon with a front window and the tailgate window open slightly for better air circulation.

Aging and Butchering

Once your deer is back at camp, at home, or at your car — if the ride home is going to be long — it's time to consider aging of the meat and preservation of the meat during aging. I prefer my meat aged, and it doesn't much matter whether it's venison or beef. It is true that meat will age somewhat in the freezer, but the rate of aging is much reduced, and I don't want to have to wait until Labor Day for last year's venison steaks. Figure 14–1 shows the approximate aging time for deer based on the highest temperature recorded during the day. For example, if during the day the temperature is getting up to a high of 50 degrees, an aging time of approximately five days (give or take one day) is about right. If the temperature is too high or if you don't have a good place to hang your deer, many butchers and meat processors will rent you a hook in one of their coolers for a nominal fee, and they can give you a recommendation on aging time based on the temperature of the cooler.

Unless the temperature is very high and cooling of the meat is critical, age your deer with the hide left on it. The hide protects the meat from dirt and insects and prevents formation of the dry,

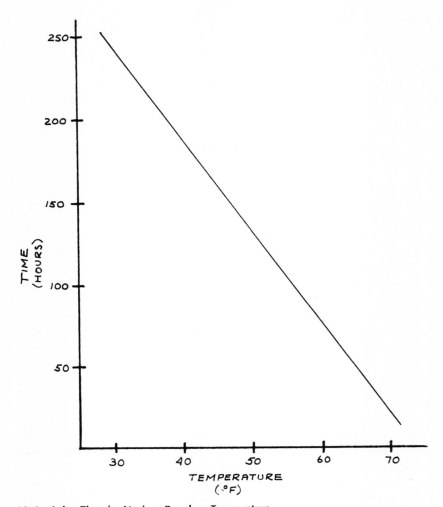

14–1   Aging Time for Venison Based on Temperature

hard crust that would otherwise develop on the exposed surfaces. If the carcass is to be hung in camp, there is a distinct danger of insects, birds, or animals getting into it. The birds and insects can be deterred by placing a cheesecloth sack around the hanging carcass. If no cheesecloth is available, the most common nuisance, blowflies, can be eliminated by sprinkling the exposed inner surfaces of the body cavity with black pepper. Animals can be discouraged by hanging the carcass as high as possible. If it is necessary to leave the carcass unattended while you go back to camp for help, some animals, such as coyotes, can be scared away by human scent, and it is a good idea in such circumstances to leave a "scent piece," such as a sweaty handkerchief, around your kill to help ward off animal predators.

More permanent deer camps often have such elaborate game-hanging facilities as high lift blocks and tackle or well-elevated game poles from which to hang the kill. In warmer areas, these hanging facilities often take the form of small screened-in buildings that provide shade and protection from animals, birds, and insects.

When it comes to butchering a deer, most hunters are pretty inept. I suppose this isn't too surprising when you consider that the average hunter gets to practice his deer-butchering skills once a year if he's lucky and somewhat less frequently if he's not so lucky. Rather than see a good carcass that's been properly cleaned and cared for ruined by an amateur butchering job, I'd be inclined to believe that a commercial butchering service is a wise investment for most hunters. The butcher or processing house will charge a fee of between ten and twenty dollars, and the result will be a professionally butchered pile of meat, ground, cut, sliced, tied, wrapped, and marked according to your instructions. Or at least it will be done according to your instructions if you are careful. Make sure that you are dealing with a reputable firm or individual, preferably one with whom you are personally acquainted and where you have done business before. If you have to go to a stranger, ask around first. The word gets around pretty quickly among the hunters in a community about where you should have your deer butchered. And make sure that your instructions to the butcher are clear. I have found, for example, that my concept of what constitutes a thick steak and the concept entertained by most butchers differ considerably. To me, a thick steak is at least one-and-a-quarter to one-and-a-half inches thick. Most butchers seem to think that three-quarters of an inch is thick. It pays to give clear instructions.

When you talk to the butcher or processor, he will probably recommend his standard cuts and butchering method, but he can probably also give you some good suggestions based on the size of your deer, its age, and where it was hit. I have only one thought to offer here. Don't convert everything into burger. Venison roasts, steaks, and chops are all genuine delights. Any butcher or hunter who would, willfully, knowingly, and with malice aforethought, convert all those delicious cuts into burger should be deprived of his meat grinder for a period of no less than one year.

When I was living near Newburgh, New York, I had the rare convenience and distinct pleasure of knowing a butcher who would make house calls. The butcher, Jerry by name, worked during the day at a job where 90 percent of his time was spent converting halves of beef into table fare. When you saw Jerry work, you knew you were watching a pro. He would come to your house carrying a large carpenter's toolbox in one hand and a butcher-block cutting board in the other. We usually set him up in business in the garage. In about five minutes Jerry would have his tools out of the box and laid out alongside his work area and have his white apron on. That man could skin a deer faster than any other man I've seen. Yank, pull, zip, zip, and the hide was gone. From then on, Jerry was a veritable maestro with saw, knife, and cleaver. A virtuoso with twine and freezer paper. No need for power tools, just hand craftsmanship. Between forty-five minutes and an hour later there would be nothing left but a pile of waste and a big beautiful stack of venison ready for freezing. You may not be lucky enough to have a Jerry around to make house calls, but the merits of paying to have your deer butchered are definitely worthy of consideration.

If you are still bound and determined to butcher your own deer, proceed as follows if you are not going to have the head mounted. If the head is to be mounted, see the following section before beginning the butchering operation.

First, the hide must be removed. To do so, hang the deer by its head or antlers at a height where you can still reach the head. If the hindquarters drag on the ground, you may have to lift the carcass higher as the skinning proceeds. Make a circular cut through the hide and into the flesh completely around the deer's neck just below the jaw; in other words, as high up the neck as possible. Then make a straight cut (slightly into the neck) down the front center of the neck and extend this cut down the chest until it meets the belly cut. Starting with the point where this straight cut joins the circular cut around the neck, work the hide loose from the flesh. This can be done with the fingers and a fair amount of pulling and tugging. Work three or four inches of hide loose all the way around the neck. Then, working from the back of the deer, grasp the loose flap of hide securely with two hands and pull down with all your weight. (Make sure the carcass is securely hung or you're liable to find yourself in a heap on the ground with a deer on top of you.) The hide will reluctantly pull away from the neck, and with occasional assists from your knife, you should be able to get it down to the base of the neck.

Now it's time to deal with the legs. Take one of the forelegs and make a girdling cut around the leg at the knee joint. Make this cut as deep as possible. With a few judicious twists and a little more assistance from your knife, the lower portion of the leg can be cut off at this joint. Once this is done, repeat the process on the other three legs.

Make a cut through the hide down the inside of the four legs to the belly cut. These cuts must go all the way from the belly cut to the point where the leg was cut off.

Now continue with the skinning. Using the cuts just described, pulling the hide down the carcass, and working it around the legs, it is possible to remove the hide in one piece. When you see flesh starting to cling to the hide, a little help from your skinning knife will serve to get the hide and flesh separated and peeling properly. Elevate the deer as necessary to keep the carcass hanging at a convenient height. A block and tackle or pulley will come in handy here. When you get to the point where only the tail is holding the hide on, wrap the thumb and forefinger around the bony flesh at the base of the tail and give a good pull. The bony column of the tail will slide right out of the hide. Lay the hide aside for now (more about it later). Snip off the bony tail at its base and discard it. Lay out a clean piece of plastic or butcher's paper beneath the deer and lower the carcass onto it. At the point where you made the girdling cut around the neck for skinning purposes, cut all the way through the neck with your knife. Cut as deeply as possible into the spinal column between two vertebrae. By twisting the head around and doing a little more cutting, you will be able to cut the head off. If you run into difficulty, use a saw to cut the spinal column. A plain old carpenter's crosscut or rip saw meant for cutting wood will do quite nicely, although it may need to be sharpened by the time you finish. You now have one dehided carcass ready for butchering. The foregoing steps may have to be accomplished by you even if you plan to use commercial butchering services, since many commercial establishments simply refuse to do the skinning job.

Before describing the butchering process, let me digress for a moment and describe a quick and simple skinning method that is applicable if the deer is to be skinned within an hour or two of when it was shot. This method is sometimes employed in the South and Southwest where it is more common to skin deer immediately after killing to aid in rapid cooling of the carcass. This method is known as the "golf-ball" or "rolling-stone" technique.

Prepare the carcass as described above to include the girdling neck cut, the front neck cut, cutting off the legs, and the inside leg cuts. Then make sure that the deer is securely tied by the antlers or upper neck to either a stout limb or some other secure object such as the trunk of a tree by a short piece of rope. Proceed with skinning the neck as described above until from eight to ten inches of hide are loosened. Then take a round stone approximately the size of a golf ball and place it inside the loosened flap of hide in the back of the neck. Bunch the hide around the rock until the rock stands out like a big lump under the hide. Tie a rope around the rock. The rock simply provides a secure tie-on point from which the rope can be pulled without tearing the hide. Tie the other end of the rope to the front bumper of a vehicle, and while one man stands by with a knife to keep the hide peeling evenly, the driver slowly backs the vehicle away. If the carcass is still fairly warm, the hide will peel away smoothly and evenly.

Regardless of which of the foregoing methods you use to skin the hide, if all of the preparatory work to include removal of the head and legs has been accomplished, the carcass is now ready for butchering. Set yourself up with a clean work space free of blowing dust, falling leaves, and other contaminants. It is important that the whole operation be conducted in as clean, neat, and professional a manner as possible. Great pains must be taken to insure that bone chips, marrow, hair, and other undesirable matter be eliminated meticulously from the final product. Only through such care will the final product be the succulent and attractive table fare that it should be.

For tools, you will need a sharp knife, a sharpener, a hatchet or cleaver, and a bone saw or carpenter's saw. I usually use two knives—a medium-weight hunting knife for the coarse work and a narrow filleting knife for the fine work. For a sharpener, I like the foolproof kitchen type that rests on the table and allows you to tune up the edge of the knife with a few quick passes through the sharpener. In the midst of slicing up a carcass, I don't want to be delayed by a fancy honing operation. A roll of freezer paper and tape, a roll of butcher's twine, and a marker to mark the wrapped meat are a must. A cutting board may also be handy, depending on your working surface. If you have any questions about the cleanliness of your working surface, cover it with taped-down freezer paper.

There are two basic ways of butchering a deer: the standard way and filleting or boning. I will begin by describing the standard method in detail and then will give a brief overview description of the boning method.

Begin the standard butchering method with the deer hanging by its hind legs. As you observe the deer from the back, there is a natural line running down the center of the spine. Cut down this line with your bone saw or wood saw from the tail to the point where the front shoulders join the neck. Then, using your knife, make a right-angle cut to the right and another to the left just in front of the shoulders. These cuts will leave you with three major pieces: the neck, and the right and left carcass halves.

The next job is to reduce the right and left carcass halves into more manageable pieces for butchering. The shoulder (front leg) can be torn loose from the body with a minimum of selective cutting. The muscles tend to separate easily, and there is no need to cut through any bone in this step. To remove the hindquarter, cut through the flank along the forward edge of the haunch until you hit the spine. Saw through the spine and lift off the haunch. Repeat these operations for the other half, and you will have three major sections to deal with from each carcass half: the shoulder or fore-quarter, the ribs, and the haunch or hindquarter.

Lay all of these sections aside except for one forequarter, and continue your butchering operation on it. The meat below the joint should be boned and laid aside for stew meat or ground meat. It usually works best to lay out two pans, one for stew meat and one for ground meat; so that as you are working, the pieces can be read-ily tossed into the appropriate pan. I am a stew fancier and have a bias toward minimizing the ground meat yield and maximizing the stew meat yield. These butchering operations are also carefully ob-served from start to finish by my dog and two cats, and there are al-ways a few scraps that manage to fall their way.

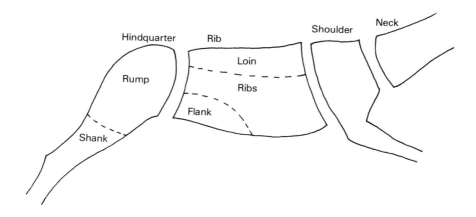

14–2 If the butchering process described in the text is used, once the neck is removed each carcass half will produce three major sections as shown here: hindquarter, rib, and shoulder or forequarter. The hindquarter produces rump roast or steaks from the rump, and stew meat or ground meat from the shank. The rib yields chops, loin roasts, spare ribs, jerky strips, and flank roast or stew meat from the flank. The upper shoulder is gen-erally converted into roast and small steaks, and the lower shoulder is used for stew meat or ground meat. The neck is trimmed for either ground meat or stew meat.

The lower part of the upper front leg bone will yield three or four small steaks from one-and-a-quarter to one-and-a-half inches thick. These steaks (shoulder steaks) are produced by making three or four girdling cuts all the way around the leg and all the way through to the bone. The bone is then cut with the saw. If you prefer a roast to small steaks, this section can be boned, rolled, and tied into a roast.

A word of caution is in order here about trimming. I prefer, where possible, to separate muscles and to bone roasts by pulling the meat and causing the muscles to separate along natural boundaries wherever possible. This method of butchering will often expose the membranes that separate the muscles. These membranes should be peeled off whenever possible. They give a somewhat unpleasant taste to the meat and tend to be tough and chewy. Care should also be taken to trim away the blood-gorged meat around bullet wounds. It is sometimes possible to recover such meat by soaking it in a diluted water and vinegar solution (fifty to one) overnight, but it is usually not worth the effort.

The only remaining effort on the forequarter is removal of the shoulder roast from the shoulder blade. This is done by cutting down to the ridge of the shoulder blade along its entire length. Then continue pulling and cutting the meat off the blade all the way around both sides. You will wind up with a flat slab of meat and a naked shoulder blade. Discard the bone and tightly roll and tie the shoulder roast.

Next tackle one of the haunches. The haunch is similar to the forequarter in that the meat below the joint is used for stew or ground meat and the upper portion is used for roasts or steaks. After removing the meat from the calf for stew or ground meat, cut the bone off just above the joint with a saw. If steaks are your preference, you can now cut five to seven decent steaks off the upper leg bone using exactly the same method described earlier for the forequarter. If you don't want any steaks, most of the remaining meat can be peeled off the upper leg by tearing along the natural muscle seams. Cut any joining ligaments with your boning knife and cut loose the tendons and membranes that attach the meat to the bone. As described earlier, peel off any attached membranes. Some of the resultant pieces of meat will be slabs that must be rolled and tied; others will be squarish chunks (haunch or rump roasts) that can be wrapped and frozen as they are.

The last section of the half to be butchered is the rib section. Take one of the two rib sections and place it on the table in front of you with the outer side up. Behind the rearmost rib is a large flap of meat attached to the spine with no ribs running through it. Cut directly behind the last rib all the way to the spine, and then trim this piece of meat away from the spine. Carefully trim away any membrane and dried-out meat. Lay this flap of meat on the table, roll it up tightly, and tie it, and you have a loin roast. Depending on family size and deer size, you may want to cut this piece in half for two roasts.

Take the remaining piece of rib section and turn it over, so the outside is down on the table. Imagine a line running parallel to the spine approximately eight inches from it. Using a cleaver or hatchet, chop the ribs along this line. If you prefer, a saw can also be used for this operation. The spine with the meaty portion attached will be converted into chops. The lower section of the ribs can be cut into convenient sections for use as spare ribs, or can be trimmed for ground meat or jerky. To produce chops from the long, meaty section of the spine, carefully cut between the short sections of rib all the way to the spine. Place a cleaver in the rearmost knife cut, rap it with a mallet or piece of wood, and a chop will drop off the end. Repeat the process until the entire section has been converted into chops.

The steps described above should now be repeated on the shoulder, rib, and haunch sections cut from the other carcass half. Once this is done, only the neck will remain to be butchered. The neck can be trimmed for either stew meat or ground meat. My preference is stew meat.

Your butchered deer should be carefully wrapped in freezer paper and tightly taped to get out as much trapped air as possible, to make the package airtight, and to prevent freezer burns. Prior to wrapping, give a final inspection for hair, bone chips, or other undesirable matter that may have slipped by you during the butchering process. Indicate on the freezer paper the cut of meat enclosed and the year of kill. If you get more than one deer, identify the packages as to deer number one, deer number two, etc. Come eating time, you will want to know if this cut is from the fat eight-pointer from the corn field or the scrawny spikehorn from the oak stand. I usually have the ground meat ground by a local butcher and either have him mix in some beef suet or mix it half and half with chopped beef. Ground venison is a little lean for my tastes, and it tends to dry out too much in the cooking unless some fat is added.

The butchering technique described in the preceeding paragraphs is what I call the "conventional" method of butchering. There are many variations on the theme, but it closely approximates the most widely used approach to butchering deer. There is another method known as "filleting." In this method, the meat is completely removed from the bones, and a fairly intact deer skeleton is discarded. It is an interesting and different approach, and I refer readers who think they might like to try this method (or at least look into it) to an illustrated article in the November 1973 issue of *Outdoor Life* magazine.

Caring for Trophies

If your kill is of such proportions that you would like to have it mounted, care should be taken right from the beginning to avoid damage to the trophy that cannot be repaired by a taxidermist. If the carcass is to be cleaned and transported before the cape and antlers are removed, don't run the belly cut further forward than the breastbone. (The cape is the hide of the head and neck and is supplied to the taxidermist for mounting.) With a little probing, pulling, and reaching, enough of the innards can be removed with limited cutting to suffice for a short time. Also take care in transporting your deer to avoid damage to the antlers or to that part of the hide that will be part of the mount. Particular care should be taken to avoid damage to the delicate areas around the eyes and mouth when dragging the carcass through brush and brambles. If any blood gets on the hide, wipe it off quickly with cold water. This is doubly important if the blood gets on any white areas.

If you are like most whitetail deer hunters, you will be able to get your trophy to the taxidermist within a few days and will be able to deliver it in person without having to resort to the U.S. mails. If this is true in your case, you can use a much simplified method of removing the cape and antlers that does not involve actually skinning out the head and face yourself.

There are two general ways to skin out the neck and cut off the head: one method is casing, and the other is slitting the back of the neck. With either method, I find it easiest to hoist the carcass good and high with the head down. Try to get the front shoulders about five feet off the ground and the antlers clear of the ground. If you can't get the carcass this high, the entire operation can be done on the ground, but it is easier if the carcass is hanging.

One of the most common mistakes that hunters make in removal of trophies is to cut the neck too short. Short neck mounts don't look very lifelike; and if your trophy has a big rack, it will be impossible for the taxidermist to mount it so that the antlers clear the wall unless you give him plenty of neck with which to work. Whether you are casing the neck or going to slit the back, once your deer is hanging the first cut is a girdling cut around the shoulders. This cut should go just through the hide and should extend from the shoulder on one side, straight up over the shoulder blade, across the back, and down the opposite side to a similar point on the opposite shoulder. This cut should be so far back that it includes some hide from the forward portion of the front legs. If you have any doubt about whether or not you are cutting back far enough, cut back farther. Better safe than sorry with a once-in-a-lifetime trophy. To extend the cut across the chest, extend the first

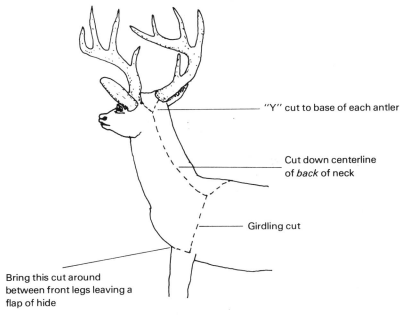

"Y" cut to base of each antler

Cut down centerline of *back* of neck

Girdling cut

Bring this cut around between front legs leaving a flap of hide

14–3 Careful removal of the cape and antlers is important if a first-class mount is to be obtained. The long cut down the deer's neck must be on the back of the neck so that the taxidermist's stitching will not show. Be sure to bring the long cut all the way back past the shoulder blades before beginning the girdling cut. Next bring the girdling cut around the front legs and then back down the animal's chest so that a flap of hide is taken off the chest. The taxidermist needs plenty of material to work with if he is to produce a lifelike head-and-shoulders mount. Too short a neck will give the appearance of a deer that ran his head through your wall.

cut around to the inside of the leg at its base and then rearward about five or six inches. Do this on both sides and then connect these two cuts with a cut across the chest. The intent of this procedure is to leave attached to the base of the neck the flap of skin that extends rearward between the two front legs and covers the chest. This piece of hide is important for a full head-and-shoulder mount.

You now have an irregular girdling cut that goes completely around the carcass. Beginning at any convenient point, such as the flap on the chest, start peeling the hide down the neck. As you work the tube of skin (this is the casing method) down the neck, you will need an occasional assist from your skinning knife at stubborn points. When you have rolled the skin down the neck to the point where the neck joins the skull, cut through the flesh of the neck all the way to the spine. Cut between two adjacent vertebrae, or the uppermost vertebra and the skull, as best you can with a knife. With a few good twists of the head, a little more assistance from your knife, and a few cuss words the head should snap right off. Deliver it just as it is, with the neck hide attached, to the taxidermist.

If you cannot hang the carcass high enough, you will find the casing method quite difficult. In such a situation, make one more cut extending from the previously described girdling cut up the back of the deer's neck. This will facilitate skinning. Start this cut at the center of the girdling cut between the deer's shoulder blades and run it up the back of the neck to a point several inches short of the antlers. At this point extend the cut in Y fashion to the base of each antler. Proceed with the skinning and head removal as described above, and deliver the head, cape, and antlers to your taxidermist. If the delivery to the taxidermist must be delayed, the entire head, cape, and antler package can be frozen without harming it. A good basic rule to remember is that if the carcass or trophy has deteriorated to the point where it has become inedible, it is also probably unmountable.

Some hunters, especially bow hunters, hunt during seasons when some or all of the racks are still in velvet. A rack in velvet is an interesting and unusual trophy, but it needs some special care. The problem with velvet antlers is that the antler is still growing, the interior is soft, and it is full of liquids and blood that will turn rancid if not quickly treated. The velvet itself is delicate and should be protected from physical damage. Velvet antlers should not be grasped roughly nor used as handles for moving or dragging the carcass. The hunter who anticipates encountering velvet racks should take a pint of formaldehyde and a hypodermic needle along with him. As soon as possible after the kill, fill the hypodermic needle with formaldehyde, push it into one of the soft antler tips, and slowly inject the fluid. In an ideal case, the formaldehyde will eventually start to trickle out near the base of the antler telling you that complete penetration has been achieved. Repeat the process at each antler tip and in the soft areas around the forks. Caution: always wear goggles or glasses when injecting formaldehyde into antlers since it has a funny way of squirting out of the antler at unexpected places. Formaldehyde in the eyes is bad news! If you do get some in your eyes, rinse immediately with water. It's also a good idea to soak velvet antlers overnight in a solution of one part formaldehyde to thirty parts of water. This will allow additional formaldehyde penetration and soaking of the velvet itself with formaldehyde. Take the antlers out of the solution the next day and allow them to dry in a cool place. The cape and antlers can now be delivered to the taxidermist, and when he is through your velvet trophy will last indefinitely.

If you do not have a taxidermist close to where you live, or if you are hunting in a remote area, you may have to completely skin out the head yourself. This is tricky job that is best left to the experts, but you may someday find yourself in a situation where you have to do it to preserve a real trophy head. Since it's a skill worth knowing, I recommend that you practice it once or twice first on some deer that are *not* going to be mounted.

If you are going to skin out the head, start by removing the cape and head from the carcass using the slit-up-the-back-of-the-neck and the Y cut previously described. Next work the hide away from the base of the antlers. It pulls away fairly readily and can best be separated using the end of a green twig about the size of a pencil. When you get to the ears, cut the cartilage off near the skull, being careful not to sever the hide. Continue to work the hide forward along the cheeks and forehead. Around the eyes and tear ducts work with your fingers between the hide and the skull and try to keep the knife between your fingers and the skull to avoid inadvertently cutting through the eyelids or tear ducts. Be sure to get about an inch of hide inside the nostrils and lips to give the taxidermist the material that he needs for a first-rate job. Once the hide is removed, skin the cartilage out of the ears by turning the ears inside out and rolling the ears back over the cartilage. This job may be facilitated by placing a stick the size of your thumb into the ear and rolling the ear back over it.

Lay the hide out on a flat surface with the hair side down. Liberally sprinkle the raw side of the hide with between half a pound and a pound of noniodized salt. Carefully work the salt into all cracks and crevices. Slit the fleshy part of the lips from the inside and work in the salt. Lay the salted hide out to dry for a day or two to dry and cure. Then resalt, roll the hide up, and it is ready to be shipped. Since the hide will probably drip somewhat, place it in a plastic leaf bag to avoid a soggy package in the mail.

To prepare the antlers for shipment, simply cut them from the skinned-out skull with a single horizontal cut that extends from about an inch and a half behind the antlers through the tops of the eye sockets. Scrape out any brains that are inside the portion of the skull attached to the antlers, salt this cavity, and the antlers are ready to go.

I have found over the years that most of the deer I get don't deserve a full-blown mounting by a taxidermist. Yet even little spikes and forkhorns can be converted into attractive wall decorations that over the years grow in number and provide nostalgic reminders of bygone hunts and campfires. The mounting process involves only the mounting of the antlers and is a job that you can do yourself for a few dollars.

First cut the antlers off the skull as described above, leaving a piece of skull about five inches by five inches attached. Since you are not mounting the head, there is no need to skin the head, and you can just cut right through the hide. Once the skull piece and antlers are removed, clean the brains out of the back of the skull and skin off the hide. This will leave you with a fairly clean piece of skullbone and antlers. Set this piece aside and let the skullbone dry out for about a month before mounting on the plaque.

While the skull and antler piece is drying out, begin making your plaque. The plaque can be made from any kind of wood that will complement the decor of the room in which you plan to hang it. I generally use white pine and stain it walnut. The size of the plaque depends on the size of the antler and skull piece with seven inches wide by seven inches high being average for a small rack. Shape the plaque to suit yourself. I find the shape of the blade of a spade to be easy to cut out with a jigsaw, yet fairly pleasing. Running a router around the edge of the plaque also gives a pleasing finished appearance to the plaque. Stain the plaque if you desire, and apply from six to eight coats of high-gloss varnish, then wet sand between the last two or three coats to give it a fine professional appearance.

In addition to the antlers, I like to mount two other objects on the plaque. One is a brass nameplate about one-and-a-half by three inches telling when, where, and by whom the deer was killed. Such a nameplate can be obtained in any trophy supply store for a few dollars and is the single biggest expense in this project. The other object that I like to add to the plaque is a depowdered deprimed cartridge, Minié ball, or broadhead of the type with which the deer was shot.

Before mounting the antlers on the plaque, sand or file the back of the skull down so that it is flat and even and will mount evenly on the board. One way to do this is to take the dried antlers and skull piece and rub it back and forth on a piece of coarse sandpaper laid face up on a table. If you have a belt sander, the job can be greatly speeded up by placing the sander on its side and pressing the back side of the skull against it. To fasten the antlers to the plaque, use two wood screws from the back of the plaque into a thick portion of the skull. Predrilled pilot holes in the back of the skull will help keep it from splitting. Once the antlers are mounted, the skull portion can either be covered with felt or leather and tacked around the edges with attractive upholstery tacks or it can be left bare. I prefer to leave the skull bare. It can be made much more attractive by bleaching the skull before mounting. To do this, simply make a mixture of equal proportions of water and liquid laundry bleach. Fill a shallow bowl about one inch deep with this mixture and set the skull and antler piece in the bowl in such a way that the skull is covered but the mixture does not get on the antlers. Let the piece stand this way overnight, take it out, and let it dry for a day or two before mounting.

Once the antlers are screwed to the plaque, glue, tack, or otherwise secure the nameplate in place. The cartridge can either be fastened from behind the plaque with a wood screw or machine screw into a predrilled hole in the case, or it can be glued in place with silicon cement. The final product will be a handsome and inexpensive wall decoration that over the years will furnish fond memories of a successful hunt.

Whether you decide to mount the head or not, there will probably be enough hide left to make tanning of the hide worthwhile. The salting, drying, and packing of hides was described earlier in the discussion of how to prepare a trophy head to be mailed. The same procedure should be used when preparing a hide for shipment to a tanner. Tanneries can be found in the classified sections of many outdoor magazines. Most of these tanneries will tan a hide with the hair on or off. Hair-on hides can be used as decorative accents or conversation pieces in places where they do not get much wear. Deer hair is brittle, falls out easily, and does not wear well. Tanned hides can be made into any number of buckskin (or doeskin) garments and accessories. Buckskin jackets, carcoats, and gloves for men or women are beautiful, comfortable, and long lasting and give the hunter the satisfaction of more complete utilization of his kill.

It should also be mentioned that the antlers and hooves can be converted into hat and gun racks. If the hooves are to be used for this purpose, you can do the job yourself, but you are probably better off letting a taxidermist do it for you. If you don't care to mount the antlers, they can be converted into handles for hunting knives, handles for pocket knives (by cutting into slabs), buttons, and many other useful items.

15

Cookery

All that has gone before in this book has been prologue. Now we come to the important part—the eating.

If you want to get maximum eating pleasure out of your venison, there are several simple rules you should follow. First, take proper care of the venison in the field and in the butchering process. Venison that was ruined before it got to the freezer cannot be salvaged in the kitchen. Second, note that venison can be used in many recipes directly in place of beef. In some cases it may be necessary to add a little fat to the recipe to account for the lack of fat in the venison, which is a low-fat, low-cholesterol meat. It is not necessary to go to wild and exotic recipes to disguise any "gamey" taste. Third, always serve the meat warm. Venison has a way of becoming much less appetizing when cold. Try warming the plates and keeping seconds in the oven. Fourth, don't overcook your venison and turn it into shoe leather. Venison dries out quickly when overcooked. With steaks, for example, try thicker cuts and keep pouring the sauces back over the meat. Fifth, carefully trim off as much fat and membrane as possible from any cut before cooking. Venison fat and membranes sometimes impart an undesirable flavor.

If you follow these five simple rules, your venison recipes are guaranteed to be a roaring success. Venison has a unique and delicate flavor all its own. Don't expect it to taste like beef. For that matter, don't expect it to taste like pork, lamb, veal, rabbit, or tuna fish. It's venison. Like recipes for any kind of meat, the variations are limitless. You will no doubt want to experiment with and develop recipes of your own. The recipes listed below are just a few of the ones that my wife and I have collected over the years and I include them here not as a comprehensive list but as a point of departure for your own experimentation. The following recipes have become particular favorites around my house, and I hope that at least a few of them become favorites of yours.

Venison Burger

Venison burger can be used in all the various dishes that normally call for beef burger. Some of the recipes that follow call for burger as an ingredient. Therefore, for openers, let's mix up some venison burger.

Start with clean, carefully trimmed venison cut into two-inch chunks or smaller. Get the beef suet you need from your local butcher.

> 5 pounds venison cubes
> 1 pound suet cubes
> garlic powder

Run the venison and suet cubes through a meat grinder, alternating venison with suet. Season with garlic powder to taste. Make sure that the resultant ground meat is thoroughly mixed. Wrap in one- or two-pound packages in either bulk or patty form and freeze. And the next time you decide to have a family cookout, try some of these delicious burgers cooked over a bed of charcoal. Or try this burger in place of hamburger in any of your favorite casseroles, meat loaves, etc.

Pennsylvania Venison Roast

This recipe was taught to me by a friend whose family had learned it years ago in Pennsylvania Dutch country. It can be used on any roast, but I always liked it best when cooked for large groups and the cut used was a large piece such as an entire upper hindquarter from the knee to the hip. The low cooking temperatures involved might seem like placing the meat on the hood of your car to cook in the bright sunlight. But the long cooking just gives the basting sauce plenty of time to soak in and mix with the natural succulent venison flavor.

To make the sauce, melt and blend the following in a saucepan:

½ cup butter
½ cup water
2 tablespoons vinegar
1 tablespoon Worcesteshire sauce
1 teaspoon sugar
1 teaspoon salt
1 chopped onion

Use this sauce for basting and serve with the roast.

Pick any roast you like as the main course, and cook at 275 to 300 degrees. Cook for twenty-two minutes per pound plus one hour. For example, a five-pound roast should be cooked for two hours and fifty minutes. Serve with boiled potatoes, buttered corn, and sweet-and-sour red cabbage for a meal that will quickly become a tradition by popular demand around your house too.

Vermont Holiday Season Meatballs

Here's one of those dishes that's meant to be used as a snack or as hors d'oeuvre but has a way of becoming a meal for anyone who stands around the chafing dish a little too long.

Mix and knead the following into a cohesive mixture in a bowl:

2 pounds venison burger
2 eggs
½ cup unseasoned breadcrumbs
salt and pepper to taste

Add a slight amount of water if necessary to moisten the mixture. Form into small meatballs, fry in oil, and drain. The real secret lies in the sauce. In a small saucepan, melt and blend

14 ounces of chili sauce
14 ounces of grape jelly

Once the sauce is completely mixed and is simmering, add the meatballs and allow to simmer until the meatballs absorb the flavor of the sauce. This dish can be made up a day or so ahead of time and kept in the refrigerator and reheated for serving. When the time comes to serve, set out in a chafing dish with toothpicks nearby and stand back.

Trapper's Jerky

Preserving meat by drying is a technique that has been employed by man for centuries. Jerked venison cannot compare in flavor to frozen meat thawed and cooked, but it is an interesting variation and one that produces great snacks for long hikes.

Start with thin steaks that are about half an inch thick. Cut strips six to ten inches long and half an inch wide from the steaks. Cut across the grain. If you use some other cut of meat, such as the strips between the ribs, or if you do not cut across the grain, the jerky will still turn out all right, but it will be tougher. Be sure to trim off all the fat, gristle, and membrane, as they don't dry out well.

Lay several pounds of the venison strips out on a table and sprinkle liberally with a mixture of salt, pepper, and barbecue seasoning. Pound the meat with a meat hammer to tenderize the strips and to work in the seasoning. Turn the strips over and repeat the process.

Next blanch the strips by dipping them in boiling water. Ten to fifteen seconds will suffice. The strips can then be hung outside to dry for three to six days in bright sunlight or hung in an oven at 150 degrees for about seven hours. The strips will dry a rich brown color and will withstand some bending without breaking when properly dried. The jerky can then be stored in any airtight container. Several pieces can be wrapped in plastic or foil, stuck in your pocket, and taken with you when you head out for a day of hunting. A couple of pieces of jerky and a drink of spring water make a great pick-me-up after a long stalk or several hours on stand.

He-Was-Slippin'-Past-My-Stand-but-I-Nailed-Him-at-the-Big-Oak-Tree Stew

Here's my favorite way of preparing venison. This stew is guaranteed to bring everyone back for seconds, and when served with warm French bread and soft butter, it just can't be beat.

Start with:

> 1 pound venison, cut into chunks
> 3 tablespoons shortening
> 1 medium onion, cut into large chunks
> 4 cups water
> 4 carrots scraped and sliced
> 3 stalks of celery, cut into one-inch pieces
> 2 medium potatoes, peeled and cubed
> ½ cup tomato paste
> 1 can beef gravy
> 1 medium-size can of cut green beans
> salt and pepper
> Spice Islands Spice Parisienne
> Spice Islands Beau Monde

In a large pot, melt the shortening and brown the meat and onions over a low heat for ten to fifteen minutes. Add the water, carrots, celery, potatoes, tomato paste, and beef gravy. Drain and add the can of beans. Add seasonings to taste. Bring to a low boil and cook for thirty minutes. This recipe will serve four people or two hungry hunters. And it's even better reheated.

Index